THE
TEA PARTY
GOES TO
WASHINGTON

THE
TEA PARTY
— GOES TO —
WASHINGTON

SENATOR RAND PAUL

★ ★

with Jack Hunter

**CENTER
STREET**

Nashville • New York

Center Street
Hachette Book Group
237 Park Avenue
New York, NY 10017

www.centerstreet.com

Center Street is a division of Hachette Book Group, Inc.
The Center Street name and logo are trademarks of
Hachette Book Group, Inc.

The publisher is not responsible for websites (or their content)
that are not owned by the publisher.

Printed in the United States of America

First Edition: February 2011

10 9 8 7 6 5 4 3 2 1

ISBN: 9781455503117

LCCN: 2001012345

Acknowledgments

I would first and foremost like to thank my wife, Kelley, without whom the campaign, my victory, and this book would not have been possible. The same goes for my three sons, William, Duncan, and Robert, who continue to make me proud each day. A special thanks to Mom, Dad, Lillian, Hilton, and my entire family, whose love and support has been immeasurable.

I would also like to thank Doug Stafford and Jesse Benton for the great campaign victory that makes this book possible; Rolf Zettersten, Kate Hartson, Bob Castillo, and the team at Center Street Books for working day and night to produce the book in a timely fashion; Jack Hunter for his indispensable writing talent; John Tate and Campaign for Liberty, Jeff Frazee and Young Americans for Liberty, and the grassroots Tea Party movement across Kentucky and across America that care so much about the future of our great Republic.

There are so many people I'd like to thank that there's no way I could list them all here. Kelley and I are especially grateful to our dear friends and neighbors in Bowling Green who have supported our family from day one. The fight for constitutional government will be a long but worthy battle, something I was reminded of so many times throughout the campaign by so many people. For your encouragement and support, I am eternally grateful.

Contents

Introduction

"I have a message from the Tea Party, a message that is loud and clear and does not mince words. We've come to take our government back."

Speaking these words after winning Kentucky's Republican primary in spring 2010, I understood that my victory was part of a much larger movement. Voters outraged by massive debt, spending and an out-of-control federal government had elected a candidate the media and political establishment had deemed too unconventional—precisely because they desired a more unconventional politics. The status quo had failed. Big government had failed. On that warm May evening, Kentucky voters sent a message loud and clear: We've had enough.

So have most Americans. Facing a $13 trillion national debt, bankrupt entitlement programs and in the midst of two long and expensive wars, our federal government is busy bailing out private industry to the tune of billions of dollars, trying to "stimulate" the economy with billions more and implementing an estimated $1 trillion national healthcare program. At precisely the moment we should be cutting spending, our government just keeps cutting checks, using money that wouldn't even exist if not printed out of thin air, borrowed from China or born of endless and astronomical debt. Said President

Obama during his victory speech in 2008: "Let us ask ourselves—if our children should live to see the next century... what change will they see? What progress will we have made? This is our chance to answer that call." And answer it Obama has—with the most rapid government growth in American history, outpacing that of every president before him combined. Obama and his party continue to ask what our government should be doing "for" our children but never seem to comprehend what it's doing "to" them, saddling future generations with unfathomable debt that truly is nothing less than generational theft. Liberals keep desiring newer New Deals and greater Great Societies, while so many Americans-at-large are increasingly clamoring for something much simpler and sane—a return to the United States Constitution.

And that clamor has become deafening. Many Republicans have grown tired of establishment GOP politicians whose actions don't match their conservative rhetoric. Many Democrats who once embraced Obama are now shocked at the size and scope of his liberal agenda. Weary of both parties, independents now represent a sizeable and growing part of the electorate, and a significant percentage of Tea Party membership. In fact, some polls even have the Tea Party ranking equal or above both major parties. As many establishment GOP politicians have had to learn the hard way, the Tea Party sees no distinction between big government Republicans and big government Democrats, drawing a new dividing line between those who want to limit government and those who want it to be unlimited. As government explodes at a rate unprecedented in our history, the Tea Party's critics continue to portray the movement as too "radical." If the Constitution and common sense still have any bearing, the Tea Party isn't the least bit radical—the federal government is.

From the Founding Fathers to Barry Goldwater to my father, Ron Paul, today, conservatives have always pointed out that the primary purpose of government is to protect our liberties. Government is not supposed to coddle us or take care of our every need, one generation to the next, cradle to grave. To the extent that we have allowed this to happen—through welfare, entitlements, the nanny state—we must give Americans what's been promised to them, but also be honest about what many, particularly younger Americans, now consider empty promises. Unquestionably, we must be practical and humane in returning to a more limited, constitutional government, but make no mistake—return we must. We can't afford not to.

These seemingly old-fashioned and constitutionally conservative notions are what first compelled me to enter the political arena as I now watch my sons grow up in an America in which each successive generation continues to make larger demands on them. What both parties have saddled this country with over the decades is unfathomable. That Obama and his party have now been able to outdo and outspend even their predecessors in such a short period of time is unforgivable. Luckily, the Tea Party has been unforgiving and justifiably so, and what I told that Kentucky audience after my primary victory last spring is even truer today: "I think we stand on a precipice. We are encountering a day of reckoning."

That day of reckoning is here. The only question is: will the Tea Party be able to take down the big government politicians before those politicians take down this country? Time is of the essence, as our federal government continues to get away with things that would've made King George blush. More Americans now realize this than perhaps at any time in our history since this nation's founding. We know what our Founders thought of tyranny and today their Tea Party descendants stand liberty minded and battle ready. It's time to send Washington a message. It's time to take our government back. It's time for a second American revolution.

THE
TEA PARTY
GOES TO
WASHINGTON

1

★ ★ ★

Time for Tea

They say that the US Senate is the world's most deliberative body. Well, I'm going to ask them to deliberate upon this—do we wish to live free or be enslaved by debt? Do we believe in the individual or do we believe in the state?

Rand Paul's election night
2010 victory speech

★ COMMITTEES OF SAFETY PRESENTS ★

BOSTON TEA PARTY

SUN. DEC 14, 2008
FANEUIL HALL

RESTORE SOUND MONEY!

FEATURED SPEAKERS: **DR. RAND PAUL**

DR. EDWIN VIEIRA DR. KATHERINE ALBRECHT

JOHN McMANUS **WALTER REDDY**

JAMES JAEGER ★ PASTOR GARRETT LEAR

LYNN LANDES, JOEL WINTERS AND MANY MORE!

1-6PM, DOORS TO OPEN AT NOON! BOSTONTEAPARTY08.COM
TICKETS $17.76 - FULL DETAILS AT:

SUPPORTED BY MASSLPA.ORG · ENDORSED BY RON PAUL & THE CAMPAIGN FOR LIBERTY · POSTER (C) MICHAEL NYSTROM · REVOLUTIONARYPOSTERS.COM

November 2, 2010, was an historic night. I had been elected to the US Senate campaigning on a traditional, constitutional platform, rooted in the founding of our nation and reflecting the values of individual freedom that have always made America great. With the Obama administration barreling in the opposite direction at breakneck speed, enacting legislation that would have astounded George Washington and incurring debt that would have outraged Thomas Jefferson, my message found an eager audience not only in Kentucky but across the country. On that night, I restated my promise to voters:

> They say that the US Senate is the world's most deliberative body. Well, I'm going to ask them to deliberate upon this. The American people are unhappy with what's going on in Washington. Eleven percent of the people approve of what's going on in Congress. But tonight there's a Tea Party tidal wave and we're sending a message to them. It's a message that I'll carry with me on Day One. It's a message of fiscal sanity. It's a message of limited constitutional government and balanced budgets. When I arrive in Washington I will ask them, respectfully, to deliberate upon this—we are in the midst of a

debt crisis and the American people want to know why we have to balance our budget and they don't? I will ask them, respectfully, to deliberate upon this: Government does not create jobs. Individual entrepreneurs, business-men and -women create jobs but not the government. I will ask the Senate, respectfully, to deliberate upon this—do we wish to live free or be enslaved by debt? Do we believe in the individual or do we believe in the state?

I had defeated my Democratic opponent by a 12-point mar-gin; he had been soundly rejected precisely for representing and symbolizing Obama and his vision. Americans were not happy with the direction of the country, and voters wanted their voices heard. This was a chorus I had heard throughout the campaign, growing louder each day and more defiant with each new debt. Washington wasn't listening, but on election night, they heard loud and clear.

In any other election cycle, my becoming a US Senator would likely not have been possible. I had never run for any elected office, had entered the race against not only a state-wide elected official, but the hand-picked candidate of the most powerful Republican in America. My campaign started at 15 percent in the polls. The national Republican Party, the Kentucky establishment, K Street and virtually every power broker in Washington, DC, had all lined up to oppose me like no other candidate running in 2010. The entire political establishment had my primary opponent's back.

Luckily, the Tea Party had mine.

The Tea Party Brews

The original Tea Party took place in Boston Harbor on December 16, 1773, over a mere three-cent tax. Today we don't consider those who took part in the protests "extremists" but patriots, who in resisting the British Crown helped kick-start a necessary and just revolution.

Today's Tea Partiers are typically not accorded the same respect by our mainstream political and media establishment, even as they protest a government arguably more arrogant than that of eighteenth-century England. A tax on tea was an outrage to our ancestors. A $2 trillion deficit and $13 trillion debt has now become an outrage to their descendants. It wasn't unusual for British officials and the press to view colonists who resisted the ruling regime in less-than-flattering terms. (Similarly, as representatives of the current ruling establishment today's political and media elite have little good to say about the Tea Party.) But even in their denial and dismissive attitudes, at some point King George III and his loyalists had to sense that a change of some sort was in the air. Today, whether they like it or not, our government and its loyalists know there's something big happening at the grassroots of American politics.

I first began to sense this when I attended what many consider to be the first modern Tea Party event held on the anniversary of the original, where on December 16, 2007, over a thousand people crammed into the historic Faneuil Hall in Boston for an event in support of my father's 2008 presidential campaign. It took place during one of the worst blizzards the city had experienced in quite some time. The event featured an array of constitutional scholars and limited government advocates, and we shocked the establishment on that date by helping Ron Paul set an all-time record for online fundraising by collecting over $6 million in one day.

Something was definitely brewing.

At that time, the same political establishment that now keeps the Tea Party at arm's length had about the same tolerance for my dad and his growing movement. Ron Paul's political platform of balancing budgets, eliminating debt and championing constitutional government simply didn't fit into a presidential campaign in which the eventual nominees of both parties—both US Senators—had spent their careers exploding budgets, expanding debt and governing outside the Constitution. Fed up with a big government Republican Party and president, Americans were understandably hungry for "change" and in 2008 ended up voting for a Democratic president who promised just that. Today, many Americans have come to regret that vote, as President Obama not only continues to offer the same big government his predecessor did, but *a lot* more of it.

Early on, most of my father's supporters in 2007–2008 already didn't trust the establishment in either party, and it's no coincidence that the Tea Party today is ingrained with the same bipartisan distrust. So many politicians and pundits now think the Tea Partiers are being unreasonable in this distrust and mock them at every turn. Yet the Tea Party really can't find any tangible reasons to trust most politicians or pundits and continue to mock *them* accordingly at many events and rallies. Thankfully, the Tea Party continues to be resilient and courageous enough not to allow the establishment to laugh or lampoon them out of existence. As the keynote speaker at the grassroots event held in support of my father's campaign three years ago—dubbed the "second Boston Tea Party"—I told the audience something that remains just as true now for today's larger movement:

> I'd like to welcome you, the sons and daughters of liberty, to the revolution. They say the British scoffed at the American rabble and laughed at the Americans, their imperfect uniforms, their imperfect tactics. They laughed at retreat after retreat of the American army. They laughed right up until Yorktown. Today, you are that American rabble and that struggle—the disillusioned, the cynical, the bereaved, bereaved at the loss of liberty. The establishment in their high rise penthouse laughs at you, they laugh at us...But you know what? They're not laughing today.

The establishment probably began to quit laughing in about 2007 when grassroots conservatives became so upset over Comprehensive Immigration Reform—more accurately described as "amnesty" for some 12 million to 20 million illegal aliens—that they shut down the congressional switchboard with an avalanche of phone calls. When Obama and John McCain joined President George W. Bush in 2008 to bail out troubled banks, automakers, and even the housing market with the Troubled Asset Relief Program (TARP), grassroots conservatives vowed that the politicians who voted for these financial schemes—Republicans included—would pay a political price. Let's just say there were a number of politicians in the GOP state primaries in the spring and summer before the 2010 midterm elections that today aren't laughing one bit and will forever regret voting for TARP.

From the protest rumblings of my father's presidential campaign to the grassroots backlash against amnesty and bailouts, the different coalitions within the Tea Party came together to put their best foot forward on Tax Day, April 15, 2009, holding massive rallies nationwide that the establishment still predictably scorned but could no longer ignore. Many more events followed in the weeks and months afterward, and now, two years later, the Tea Party is not only still in full force but has proved itself an enduring movement with the potential to change American politics forever and for the better. Despite accusations to the contrary, the Tea Party is organized from the bottom up, decentralized and independent. No matter how much the establishment would love to control and manipulate this movement, its political narrative is dictated by the grass roots, not the other way around. The "rabble" has spoken and the establishment must now listen—whether they like it or not.

Taxed Enough Already

I was scheduled to coach my youngest son's little league game on April 15, 2009, when I received a call to speak at a local Tea Party event. I told the assistant coach that I wouldn't be away long, anticipating that I would arrive to a handful of folks, give a brief speech and leave twenty minutes later. But when I arrived, there were seven hundred sign-waving Tea Partiers filling Fountain Square Park in downtown Bowling Green, Kentucky. It was the largest political gathering I had ever witnessed in my town and, at that moment, it was hard to deny that something big was indeed happening. Soaking in the enthusiastic crowd and the electricity in the air, I said to the people that day:

Two hundred years ago Sam Adams and his rabble-rousers threw tea in Boston's harbor. Sam Adams famously said, "It does not require a majority to prevail, but rather an irate, tireless minority keen to set brushfires in people's minds." That's right—an irate, tireless minority keen to set brushfires. Looks like we've got one hell of a brushfire to me.

And from that day forward the Tea Party has been keen on fanning the flames, not simply as a tireless minority but as a potential majority, with some polls showing that more Americans identify with the Tea Party than either the Republican or Democratic parties. But what could Tea Partiers, to borrow from Adams, be so "irate" about? On that great, historic Tea Party day, I stated it in plain English:

We now pay more in taxes than we spend on food, clothes and housing combined. Taxes are high because spending is out of control. We are spending ourselves into oblivion. The Republicans doubled the deficit from $5 trillion to $10 trillion. The Republicans and Democrats together spent a trillion dollars bailing out the banks and then the Democrats alone spent another trillion dollars on pork barrel spending. This year we will add $1.75 trillion to the deficit. Our deficit, as a percentage of gross national product, is greater than at any time in our history. We are bankrupting this country, and the bottom line is that the politicians don't get it. The only message they will understand is a one-way ticket home. Instead of bringing home the bacon, let's bring home the politicians. Bring them home to live with the mess they've created.

I ended my speech that day with one simple line: "I'm Rand Paul and I approve this message."

The movement had certainly grown beyond just Ron Paul adherents. The Tea Party began to gather forces from every direction, from Sarah Palin fans to supporters of former Arkansas governor and presidential candidate Mike Huckabee. They all came with one grievance foremost on their mind—the national debt. This problem had become so pressing and overwhelming that it had set off brushfires in the minds of millions of Americans across the country. The "tea" in Tea Party is often said to stand for "taxed enough already" and, while the Tea Partiers in each city tended to be social conservatives for a strong national defense, unquestionably their primary motivation was driven by a sincere concern over the size and scope of the national debt.

In the beginning, the Left tried to argue that the Tea Party was little more than top-down organized publicity stunts fomented by FOX News. The reality was actually quite different and much more amazing. In Kentucky, each Tea Party started spontaneously and independent of others. To this day, statewide communication between the different Tea Parties in each city is spotty at best, and yet in city after city thousands of folks gather at local events. This has been the dynamic of the movement nationwide. When a so-called "national" Tea Party convention was held last year, state and local organizers throughout the country issued statements to make it known that there was no national organization that spoke for them.

The Tea Party sprang in each state de novo. It wasn't created by a network. It wasn't created by a billionaire. It came from the people. It has no single leader, is often adamantly against leadership and threatens the power structure of both political parties. It threatens the perquisites and privileges of the establishment and, therefore, many on both sides of the aisle think it must be destroyed. That the Tea Party has so many enemies in the establishment media and government should tell its members they're doing something right.

Open Mic Night

On the campaign trail, I always described the Tea Party as an "open mic night," or a forum to redress our grievances. It came into being to fill a niche that neither party allows—dissent. Americans who normally put in their day's work, arrive home to their spouses and kids, and go to school events and soccer games are largely ignored by Washington, but they are now worried enough to march in the streets. As much as the Left wants to depict the Tea Party as an angry mob, it is better described as a multitude of concerned and worried average citizens who have spontaneously banded together because they fear the consequences of massive overspending and debt. I've traveled thousands of miles across Kentucky over the past year, and I've met the Tea Party, one person at a time, one city at a time. They often come from different social, cultural and economic backgrounds but unite to address head-on the daunting problems facing our nation. And although they come together, they never really come together *too much*. There really is no Kentucky Tea Party—simply independent groups, organized by city, inspired by patriotism and informed by common sense.

Has there been a movement in the last hundred years where in many cities across the country people just spontaneously show up for a protest? This happened on April 15, 2009 in about ten cities in Kentucky but probably over a thousand cities nationwide. This is quite amazing when you consider that not only do the Tea Parties not communicate with one another, but they don't really communicate with anyone nationally. Each group values its own autonomy. In my experience, the Tea Party doesn't have aspirations to coalesce as a national organization in large part because they so dislike rules and authority. Tea Partiers often don't like to have politicians speak at their events because they don't want to be too attached to the political machine, unlike Republican or Democratic gatherings where the politicians do all the talking and citizens are rarely given a forum to express their opinion. Such party meetings are typically made up of a small clique of partisan insiders who jealously guard their own political turf. The Tea Party is the opposite: a large group of unabashed, nonpartisan outsiders who want everyone to have their say yet doggedly reject letting a single individual or a handful of individuals speak for them or the movement.

I said time and again throughout my campaign that the Tea Party movement equally chastises both Republicans and Democrats. Of course, this has always fit me to a tee, since my constant criticism of my own party's job performance is one of the reasons that I was not endorsed by establishment Republicans during the 2010 primary. Many conservatives were outraged over Bush's deficits and spending. They felt betrayed, and rightfully so. The dominant message of the Tea Party is fear that our national debt and budget deficit—the fault of both parties—will destroy our nation. Though the movement is heavily decentralized—and what some might call disorganized—advocating for a much smaller, leaner federal government continues to be its one unifying principle.

The extent to which the movement's critics not only dismiss grassroots voters' grievances but the Tea Party's very legitimacy is amusing. Commenting on the April 15, 2009 rallies, then House Speaker Nancy Pelosi said, "This [Tea Party] initiative is funded by the high end—we call it 'AstroTurf,' it's not really a grassroots movement. It's AstroTurf by some of the wealthiest people in America to keep the focus on tax cuts for the rich instead of for the great middle class."

There's no question that some in the political establishment have tried to latch on to the Tea Party or manipulate the movement for their own benefit. Any Tea Partier could tell you this, and they all are aware of it precisely because maintaining their independence is so important. The movement is keenly aware of possible establishment-type interlopers and, if anything, is probably overly suspicious—in fact Tea Partiers are quite the opposite of being dupes, as critics such as Pelosi love to portray them.

Pelosi's view of the Tea Party is typical of elitists. Or as pollsters Scott Rasmussen and Douglas E. Schoen, authors of the book *Mad As Hell: How the Tea Party Movement Is Fundamentally Remaking Our Two-Party System*, explained at *Politico.com:*

(T)he political class's assault on the tea parties has been continuing and systematic. Indeed, Rasmussen Reports has shown that 87 percent of the political class views "tea party member" as a negative description, while almost half—or 48 percent—of ordinary mainstream voters see it as a positive.

The reason for this broad-based support is simple: Voters in our survey said that they believe that the current leadership in both parties has failed to achieve policies that address their most pressing concerns—creating jobs and fixing the economy. Furthermore, respondents were clear that they want a pro-growth agenda, fiscal discipline, limited government, deficit reduction, a free market and a change from politics as usual. They view the tea party movement as having a unique contribution in achieving these goals.

Given today's anti-Washington, anti-incumbent sentiment, it is hardly surprising that voters have largely rejected the efforts of political, academic and media elites—on both right and left—to ignore or marginalize the tea party. Many among these elitists have now branded the tea party movement as AstroTurf, an inauthentic political movement funded by wealthy and influential businessmen.

If the Tea Party was indeed "AstroTurf" and somehow completely manufactured by the Republican Party or FOX News, then it would be a deception of epic proportions. Republicans have been promising limited government for years and have delivered nothing. Conservatives simply don't believe the Republican establishment anymore and support the Tea Party precisely because it is both outside of and in opposition to both major parties—not simply an auxiliary of the GOP. Political elites have attempted to dismiss the movement because to recognize its power and influence is a direct threat to both parties. This notion that the movement was somehow created by the Republican Party is particularly laughable when it was painfully clear in my own primary that the entire GOP establishment wished that my campaign and the Tea Party would just go away. Rasmussen and Schoen outline the movement's independence, power and popularity:

> The Tea Party movement has become one of the most powerful and extraordinary movements in recent American political history. It is as popular as both the Democratic and Republican parties. It is potentially strong enough to elect senators, governors and congressmen. It may even be strong enough to elect the next president of the United States—time will tell. But the Tea Party movement has been one of the most derided and minimized and, frankly, most disrespected movements in American history. Yet, despite being systematically ignored, belittled, marginalized, and ostracized by political, academic, and media elites, the Tea Party movement has grown stronger and stronger... demonstrating a level of activism and enthusiasm that is both unprecedented and arguably unique in recent American political history.

The Tea Party continues to endure and grow whether the establishment likes it or not. The slanders and lies political elites have directed toward the Tea Party not only have had little effect, but simply make it more attractive to countless Americans fed up with the condescending attitudes of those elites.

And not surprisingly, questioning the Tea Party's legitimacy has been only one of many attack tactics.

Left-Wing Prejudice on Full Display

As I mentioned, the Tea Party is perhaps described as an open mic night, something anyone who attends a party event would immediately understand. But it seems some who would never dare attend a Tea Party rally also see a sort of nightclub dynamic, though not in the positive manner I do. Said MSNBC's Keith Olbermann of Tea Party events: "It is as if a group of moderately talented performers has walked on stage at a comedy club on improv night. Each hears a shout from the audience, consisting of a bizarre but just barely plausible fear or hatred or neurosis or prejudice." Hatred? Neurosis? Prejudice? Each of these words better describes Olbermann and his network, and no event I've attended even remotely resembles the left-wing pundit's characterization of Tea Partiers.

Chicago Tribune syndicated columnist Clarence Page did something few mainstream columnists do—he actually attended a Tea Party event before he wrote about it. Page, who criticizes the movement as "a slogan in search of an agenda," nevertheless has effectively gauged and described its genesis: "Tea Parties lack much in the way of formal structure, leadership, or agendas because their movement is an orphan, unified by a shared sense of abandonment by Republicans and cluelessness by Democrats." Page is right. Most Tea Parties lack any formal structure, board of directors, etc. It truly is a spontaneous, grassroots movement for people to air grievances with their government. In this spirit of dissent, the Tea Party is quintessentially American, and I respect Page (even though he doesn't agree with the Tea

Party message), simply because he doesn't attempt to vilify the movement with race baiting and name calling.

The vast majority of Tea Parties are held in public squares and public parks, not convention centers and ballrooms. They don't require tickets or pre-registration. They draw all kinds of people and there are always a few there to provoke and carry offensive signs. If you get 100,000 people together there are going to be a few outliers and, in a public square or park, event organizers can't stop people from standing around and holding stupid signs.

Still, the Tea Party's critics love to characterize the entire movement by the actions of a few. Ironically, when discussing the subject of welfare, liberals are always quick to defend welfare programs despite the many recipients who take advantage of the system. When discussing Islam, respectable journalists are always careful to note that terrorists and radicals do not define that religion. But the Tea Party is regularly held to an entirely different standard, where if a few people show up—out of a crowd of thousands—with signs comparing the president to a fascist or communist dictator it becomes enough to disparage and dismiss the entire movement.

The double standard doesn't stop there. My family and I attended the first inaugural parade for George W. Bush and some of the signs were so offensive and vulgar that I had to shield the eyes of my seven-year-old son. Throughout his presidency, Bush was routinely depicted as Hitler, Stalin, Satan, you name it. Protesters bumped up against us hurling the F bomb in front of our children. It comes with the job. Does this necessarily mean that every American who might be sympathetic to anti-war protesters or who might have been critical of Bush's foreign policy is some sort of crazy person? I certainly don't believe that and, given the bipartisan nature of the Tea Party, I don't think many of its members today would be so quick to cast the same aspersion.

Most of the Tea Party's liberal critics are not so generous, attributing sinister motives to grassroots conservatives that are virtually non-existent. *New York Times* columnist Maureen Dowd wrote of a town hall protest in 2009, in which Tea Party folks were letting their voices be heard: "Instead of a multicultural tableau of beaming young idealists on screen, we see ugly scenes of mostly older and white malcontents." Is Dowd serious? Who's bringing up race here and what does it have to do with anything? Her fellow *Times* columnist Paul Krugman wrote of the same protesters that "they're probably reacting less to what Mr. Obama is doing, or even to what they've heard about what he's doing, than to who he is," adding that Tea Party anger reflects "cultural and racial anxiety." Obviously, Krugman has never attended any of the events on which he seems to consider himself an expert, and his and Dowd's opinions of the Tea Party reveal more about their own left-wing prejudices than that of the Tea Party movement.

Last summer the National Association for the Advancement of Colored People (NAACP) sponsored a resolution demanding that the Tea Party repudiate its "racist elements." The resolution defied all logic. Should, or would, the NAACP repudiate the "racist elements" in their midst, given the extreme rhetoric of figures like Rev. Jeremiah Wright or the voter intimidation of groups like the New Black Panther Party? Of course not. The NAACP has no control over these individuals or groups. The decentralized nature of the Tea Party means no one really controls the movement, much less possesses the ability to rein in or prevent the occasional, random extremist. An organization like the NAACP, which is structured, would be more capable of denouncing undesirable elements in its ranks than the Tea Party, given its lack of structure—though I won't be holding my breath for the organization to be doing any such denouncing anytime soon.

At a campaign event during the election a liberal reporter approached a member of my staff and asked him how it felt to be the only African American in the room. He was offended. So was I. So were most of my staff, including other African Americans. It was another case of liberals' own prejudices against the Tea Party dictating their perception of the movement as opposed to the reality at hand.

My experience with the Tea Party is that it's actually quite diverse, more so than the Republican Party. Almost every Tea Party I've been to has featured African-American speakers. At an event in Louisville there were ten speakers, and two were black. A black minister from the west of Louisville, who is a supporter of mine, approached me after the Rachel Maddow controversy in which the MSNBC host tried to paint me as somehow being against the civil rights movement due to my support of property rights (more on that later). The minister wanted to let me know that he believed the civil rights issue of our era was education. He was concerned about the high numbers of minority kids dropping out of school and that the education establishment seemed more worried about pandering to the unions than actually fixing our schools.

It is worth pointing out that my political philosophy, which values the importance of the individual over the collective, is the antithesis of the mind-set of not only bona fide racists but race-obsessed liberals, both of whom always see people as belonging to a group. A left-wing columnist like Maureen Dowd sees in the Tea Party "white malcontents," implying that somehow their race disqualifies their outrage—while never noticing that not all of these people are white, and they have plenty of reasons for their malcontent. The Tea Party sees only big government. It is the movement's critics who continue to see only race.

My father is fond of saying that "freedom brings people together," and this has been my experience with the Tea Party, where people of all races, backgrounds and walks of life have come together to address the pressing problems of astronomical spending and debt. The Tea Party doesn't see politics in black and white, but black and red—even as its critics continue to see racism where it simply does not exist.

The Tea Party Is Shaping the National Debate

Some have compared the Tea Party to the Ross Perot phenomenon during the 1992 presidential election, but the difference is the Perot movement actually took votes from Republicans and the Tea Party brings more votes. Both movements represent a backlash against the party establishments, but differ significantly in their results. The question has been posed as to what the Republican establishment will do with Tea Party candidates who aren't willing to toe the party line? What will Tea Party candidates do if the GOP doesn't trend more toward the movement's agenda of balanced budgets and constitutional government? Good questions both, yet it must be said that regardless of what the future holds, the Tea Party is already shaping the national debate and directing the political narrative. The Republican caucus is already talking about our debt more than they used to. Republicans are already beginning to understand that something must be done about spending. You now hear repeatedly from candidates across the country—some sincere, some not—that it is a "spending problem, not a revenue problem." I've had Republican politicians from Kentucky and across the country come up to me and say, "We're not going to mess things up again!" They claim that if the GOP gains control again, they're not going to waste their electoral victory this time.

Do they mean it? It would be easy to say "time will tell," but right now time is not a luxury. Before the midterm election, the *Wall Street Journal* published a report claiming that many establishment Republicans were cheering the Tea Party for political expediency during the elections but were prepared to compromise with the Democrats once in office. This will not do. We've been down this road before and every Republican who has claimed in the past that their particular spending bill or surrender of conservative principles was done with good intentions, must be sharply reminded how the path to hell was paved. My approach to politics is that you simply stand up for what you believe in. This should be any serious conservative's starting point. If your first impulse is to compromise, and Obama and the Democrats are far to the Left, but you start in the middle, then you'll end up somewhere between the middle and the Left. Hasn't this been the Republican Party's problem for too long and precisely the reason we now have a Tea Party?

Speaking at a Tea Party event in Paducah, Kentucky, during the campaign, I asked the crowd, "Is anyone here from the Tea Party?" The thunderous applause could have come from any number of Tea Parties, on any given day, held regularly across the country. I told the crowd, "I think we're going to have a Tea Party tidal wave...There is a day of reckoning coming, we must grab hold of our government again, and not let them spend us into oblivion." The crowd cheered and as I looked out across the audience, I could see what the establishment politicians and mainstream pundits still can't see or simply don't care to—everyday Americans, busy working jobs just to pay the bills and put food on the table, who are genuinely worried about their country's future. A Rasmussen poll released that same day showed that 81 percent of Americans thought the country was headed in the wrong direction. Such numbers are not insignificant and reflect the mood that empowers and gives influence to the Tea Party, no matter how much the mainstream media tries to downplay it.

In the weeks and months to come after announcing my candidacy for US Senate, the Tea Party's strength would be tested, stringently, strategically and on multiple levels. Would the millions of Americans clamoring for substantive "change"—not of the Obama variety and certainly not of the recent Republican brand of George W. Bush—have voices loud enough and enduring enough to carry an election with national implications?

2

★ ★ ★

My Tea Party Journey

Rand Paul's success can be understood in the genealogy of the Tea Party movement. Its viral and decentralized traits, the intellectual foundations of its libertarianism, and its fundraising tactics all come from Ron Paul's presidential campaign. The first Tea Party event of the Obama era was arguably a Ron Paul "money bomb" fundraiser...

Ben Van Heuvelen, Salon.com
May 14, 2010

★ ★ ★

As many Americans now find their voice in the Tea Party, I sort of feel like the Tea Party found me. It is not unusual for parents to inculcate their beliefs and values in their children, and my father's unwavering loyalty to the Constitution and limited government certainly made an impression on me from an early age. During my father's 2008 presidential campaign his fervent supporters would often ask me, "What's it like to be the son of Ron Paul?" I've never really known how to answer that question. What's it like *not* to be the son of Ron Paul? My dad has always been my dad and my political hero. His uncompromising stands and unwavering political philosophy inspired not only me but helped inspire what became the Tea Party movement. Dad has practically been a one-man Tea Party since the day I was born. The difference today is that he has so much company. Or should I say, we both do.

I suppose it's symbolic that I would have spoken at what some consider the first modern Tea Party in Boston in 2007, and even more appropriate that it was in support of the man whose presidential campaign many consider a precursor to today's Tea Party. Yet, it wasn't exactly the first time I took to the podium to support my dad.

My Father's Son

My first political debate was in 1984 against then Congressman Phil Gramm. It was during my father's bid for the US Senate, when he asked his twenty-one-year-old son to stand in for him while he was off in Washington for a House vote. Gramm remembers my performance graciously: "I listened to him pretty closely and I remember the young man did quite well." Even then, the debate was over adding new debt. Many fiscal conservatives were upset that even under Ronald Reagan spending was expanding more rapidly than under Jimmy Carter. Congressman Ron Paul didn't become a senator that year, but I always look back on my father's example and the opportunities he gave me as the early beginnings of my own political journey. Of course, I eventually did make it to the US Senate and can't thank my father enough for his sage advice and the moral and political foundations that have helped me in life and, now, public service. Family values have always been important to the Pauls and I couldn't have asked for better parents than Ron and Carol Paul.

My father was stationed at Kelly Air Force base in San Antonio, Texas, from 1963 to 1965. My parents ended up raising five children in Texas, most of that time spent living in Lake Jackson. It was a small town where we could ride our bikes to school, baseball practice and even swim meets—all the Paul kids were competitive swimmers. My older brother Ronnie was a two-time Texas state swimming champion. My dad had been a state champion track star. I wasn't as good as either of them but I achieved beyond my abilities, even winning the hundred-yard freestyle swim for our school district as a senior in high school. In the early 1980s, my father's friend Congressman Barry Goldwater Jr. visited during the annual political picnic, where we held a big swimming competition. Growing up, my brothers and I would always compete against our dad, but as we got older we were given the subtle hint not to win. That day, Goldwater never got the message.

The Paul kids were always taught the value of a dollar. We were expected to work hard and were never given money without earning it. There was no allowance. I was always mowing yards—our yard, the neighbor's yard, my parents' friend's yard, my parents' friend's neighbor's yard—you name it, I mowed it. My first job in high school was working at a miniature golf course, which was great because I got to stay out late since my parents didn't really know what time mini golf closed. The Pauls never were extravagant, we always shopped at Sears or JC Penney and wore inexpensive tennis shoes without thinking much about it—that is, until my little sister came along. As the youngest child, my sister, Joy, pretty much got anything she wanted and, of course, basic shoes simply would not do for her.

My parents' love and support has been unconditional and I remain very much my father's son, not only in my politics but in the way that Dad and I have different approaches to things. It really shouldn't surprise people that part of being Ron Paul's son means being your own man, independent and unique-minded. If I blindly followed Dad with no questions or differences of opinion I would be less my father's son, not more. Dad and I have always understood this even when others have not. My father's popularity and influence have been a tremendous help to my political career. I don't think I could have become a US Senator without him but, for most of my life and certainly my political life, I have never been dependent on my dad—and he wouldn't have it any other way.

While many now look to my father as a champion of liberty, let's just say I caught the liberty bug much earlier and, yes, I admit I had a particular advantage. As a child, when people would come over to the house and start political discussions, I was always very comfortable with the adult conversation. When I was younger I'd just listen, but as I got a bit older I was always anxious to participate. I used to regularly listen to my father's half of phone radio interviews. I began knocking on doors for Dad in 1974 at age eleven and would be involved in each of his campaigns until I went away to college.

Perhaps my best education concerning the rough-and-tumble world of politics came in 1976 when the entire family traveled to Kansas City for the Republican National Convention. That year, my father was one of only four US Congressmen to endorse Ronald Reagan for president.

Ron, Reagan and Me

The 1976 Republican National Convention was probably the most exciting party convention in a century. No candidate had secured the nomination before arriving at the convention and the delegates were evenly split between Reagan and President Gerald Ford. The Texas and California delegations were for Reagan and by winning the primary in those states Reagan received 100 percent of the delegates. As a tactical matter, Ford's "forces" separated the delegations of both states to opposite poles on the convention floor, where the California delegation would chant "Viva!" and the Texas delegation would respond "Olé!" Emotions were high. So high, in fact, that Vice President Nelson Rockefeller, obviously a prominent Ford backer who was seated with his New York delegation right next to the Texas folks, at one point took a swing at one of the Texas delegates with his state's floor marker (the signs convention delegates carry to identify what state they represent). Rockefeller also got into a scuffle over the use of a phone on the convention floor. As I said, emotions were high.

Ford was supported by Texas' US Senator John Tower and when Texas went for Reagan that year the delegates prevented Tower from getting floor credentials. Instead, they named my dad as the honorary head of the Texas delegation even though Ron Paul had been elected to represent that state's 22nd congressional district just a few months before. At one point Tower did come onto the convention floor with borrowed credentials, but when a Texas delegate spotted him they had security escort him away. Reagan lost the nomination that year but essentially won the party. For me at thirteen, this was all quite a spectacle to behold.

While that contentious Reagan vs. Ford presidential convention is but a distant memory for most, when I won the GOP nomination for the US Senate in Kentucky thirty-four years later it did not go unnoticed by me that those in the old guard of the Kentucky Republican Party who staunchly supported my GOP primary opponent—had also all been prominent Ford delegates in 1976.

Perhaps ironically, every Republican likes to claim the mantle of Reagan these days, sometimes out of genuine admiration, other times, pure politics. I'll always remember that much like my father today, Reagan in 1976 was considered by many establishment types to be outside the "mainstream" of the Republican Party, as evidenced by not only Ford's people but later in 1980 when presidential candidate George H.W. Bush would describe Reagan's tax-cutting proposals as "voodoo economics." Today, media pundits like to ask whether there would be a place for Reagan in the "extreme" Tea Party, bashing the supposedly "radical" movement for wanting to do things like abolish the Department of Education—forgetting that Reagan also wanted to abolish it. The left-wing media attacks Tea Party candidates as belonging to an impractical "party of no," forgetting that Reagan also saw the state, unequivocally, in negative terms, declaring that "Government is not a solution to our problems, government is the problem."

Conservatives were naturally disappointed that despite such rhetoric, government and our national debt grew exponentially under Reagan, something many Republicans like to blame on a Democratic congress or defense build-up, the latter of which increased 40 percent during his presidency. Of course, national defense is a primary function of our federal government and I believe should probably be the largest part of our budget—albeit a much smaller budget. Today, too many Democrats always want to cut the defense budget but never domestic spending, while too many Republicans always want to cut domestic spending while ignoring the defense budget. Americans who want to seriously reduce the debt, many inspired by the Tea Party, are beginning to realize we must look at the entire budget, leaving no stone unturned.

Conservatives who now compare Reagan's defense build-up during the Cold War—when we faced down a world superpower with massive nuclear capability—to the supposed need for increased defense budgets today to fight a drastically different type of enemy, do a disservice to Reagan, his legacy and common sense. Of course we all recognize the need to fully fund our military, to defend against any threats and defeat any enemies on the horizon. But we also need to recognize that America already spends nearly as much on defense as every other country on earth combined. Is this necessary? Are all of our foreign commitments necessary? What America spends on defense—and it should be asked, how much of this qualifies as actual "defense"?—accounts for almost half of total global defense spending. Is this right? We spend billion of dollars keeping and maintaining foreign bases—shouldn't our allies be shouldering some of the cost, particularly when it comes to their own defense? Much like entitlements, what we spend on our military has long been drastically out of sync with what we can actually afford, producing the same expensive results that always characterize big government. The Cato Institute's Doug Bandow details this consistent government growth:

America spends more inflation-adjusted dollars on the military today than at any time since the end of World War II. Figured in 2000 dollars, the U.S. devoted $774.6 billion to the military in 1945, the final year of World War II. In 1953, the final year of the Korean War, military outlay ran to $416.1 billion. Expenditure during the Vietnam War peaked at $421.3 billion in 1968. By contrast, in 2010—even before the Afghan surge and other unplanned expenditure—the administration expected to spend $517.8 billion. That's more than during the lengthy, but often warm, Cold War.

Reagan's massive defense build-up occurred during a different era and was done to contain a much different foe. It's somewhat absurd to compare any of the problems we face today, as many and as serious as they may be, with the magnitude of the Soviet menace; or as Daniel W. Drezner, a professor of international politics at Tufts University, explained in *Foreign Policy*:

> I'm about to say something that might be controversial for people under the age of twenty-five, but here goes. You know the threats posed to the United States by a rising China, a nuclear Iran, terrorists and piracy? You could put all of them together and they don't equal the perceived threat posed by the Soviet Union during the Cold War. And until I see another hostile country in the world that poses a military threat in Europe, the Middle East and Asia at the same time, I'm thinking that current defense spending should be lower than Cold War levels by a fair amount.

During his time, Reagan understood what problems America faced and balanced his limited government principles against the need to protect his country and its interests. Republicans today should do the same, recognizing that our time is much different than Reagan's. And, as the Tea Party now demands, conservatives must live up to their rhetoric by finally and fully limiting government—all of it.

It's amusing how often Reagan's admirers will recall his rhetoric while ignoring his actions or the context of those actions—not to mention their own. I'll never forget one aggressive old pol pulling me aside during the Republican primary at one of my first campaign appearances and saying, "Young man, we follow Reagan's Eleventh Commandment around here"—in other words, you better not criticize the party favorite in your speech. Meanwhile, the county chair begrudgingly introduced me while sporting a lapel sticker supporting the party favorite. I thought to myself, *They want me to adhere to Reagan's Eleventh Commandment?* Who do these people think they are? I was at the 1976 convention when my father was one of only four US Congressmen to support Reagan over a sitting Republican president and now these entrenched party types dare lecture me about Reagan? I thought, *Most of these people supported Ford! I should be lecturing them!* Besides, Reagan might have once said never to criticize one's fellow Republican but his supporters and Ford's people went at it tooth and nail, fighting intensely for control of the party. Believe me—I saw it firsthand.

Also, and not so surprisingly, by the end of the primary campaign nobody was talking to me about Reagan's Eleventh commandment as my GOP opponent trashed me daily and I rarely even mentioned his name. I didn't have to. The positive message and momentum of the Tea Party was enough to carry the day. We won the fight despite millions of dollars of attack ads leveled against us, and we won because I recognized the emerging power and significance of this new movement—and I had been Tea Party before Tea Party was cool.

Activism and Education

Maybe it comes from my dad, but I've always been comfortable in being an independent or an "outsider" in my conservative philosophy. In college, I joined the Young Conservatives of Texas (YCT) a spin-off of Young Americans for Freedom

(YAF), a much older and established right-leaning youth organization. The YCT group was founded in 1980 by student activist Steve Munisteri and a handful of others who broke away from YAF believing that organization was not conservative enough—something I couldn't have been accused of. Not so coincidentally, Munisteri recently emerged politically much as I did, winning the Texas Republican Party chairmanship in 2010.

I joined YCT because it was an ideological group. They believed in limited, constitutional government regardless of party affiliation. My conservatism was, and is, more philosophical in nature than partisan, and I am a Republican precisely because I believe my party is supposed to stand for particular principles rooted in liberty. In high school I cut my teeth on philosopher-novelist Ayn Rand, probably still one of the most influential critics of government intervention and champions of individual free will.

I later moved on to the Russian author Fyodor Dostoyevsky. To this day I still consider Dostoyevsky's *The Brothers Karamazov* and *Crime and Punishment* two of the greatest novels of all time. In *Crime and Punishment*, Dostoyevsky puts to narrative the common nineteenth-century belief that if there were no God, all would be permissible. Dostoyevsky's protagonist Raskolnikov acts out on that premise by killing a woman yet justifying it in his mind. He convinces himself that he will do some good with the ill-gotten proceeds and that the ends justified the means. The greatness of the book is that you can see and feel his fear leading up to the act, and you see and feel the relentless gnaw of his conscience eat away at him as he discovers that theory cannot ultimately trump conscience.

I also began to read a lot of free-market Austrian economists such as Ludwig von Mises, F. A. Hayek (Hayek's *The Road to Serfdom* is a must-read for any serious conservative) and Murray Rothbard. Commonly known as the "Austrian school," these economists are free-market champions who explain why government intervention (stimulus, bailouts, etc.) never work, and only prolong the problems such measures were intended to correct. Sound familiar? It was modern-day subscribers to Austrian economics, people like my father and Euro Pacific Capital President Peter Schiff, who predicted the housing bubble and financial crisis of 2007–2008 when virtually all the "experts" were saying just the opposite, denying that there were any problems on the horizon. Rothbard in particular, one of the major figures of the Austrian school, was a great influence on my thinking and when I was a young man I was lucky to meet him. Rothbard would come to Washington, DC, to speak to some of my father's interns in the early 1980s. I had the privilege of driving him to the airport and it was a thrill to have that one-on-one time with him. Interestingly enough, Rothbard was once a close associate of Ayn Rand.

There have been many stories floating around that I was named after Ayn Rand, but the truth is my parents named me Randal, which was later shortened to just Rand by a woman far more important to me than any writer—my wife, Kelley.

Meeting Kelley, Kentucky Bound

Kelley and I first met at an oyster roast hosted by some mutual friends in Atlanta. She was actually invited by another guy she had been dating on and off, who, to my benefit, wasn't around for most of the evening. I've often been told I look younger than my age and in 1989, when my then twenty-five-year-old future wife first saw me, she apparently thought I was too young, telling me later that she thought I might have been a teenager even though I was twenty-six. Dismissing me at first, Kelley didn't really know anyone else at the party and luckily that worked to my benefit. Kelley, an English major in college, overheard me discussing Dostoyevsky with some friends, decided maybe I wasn't as young as I looked and we struck up a conversation. Our advertising agent once asked me on camera to describe our first meeting, but I simply blushed and gave a very lame answer. Being put on the spot to talk about my emotions in public is not something that is easy for me, but one thing I will never forget about our first meeting is that I leaned forward and kissed her in the kitchen of our friend's house, in front of who knows who. I had never been so forward or daring before. I then asked for Kelley's phone number but didn't write it down, which she kidded me about. "Don't worry, I'll remember it," I said. I called Kelley the next day, we had our first date that night and the rest is history. Something special brought us together and still keeps us together over twenty years later.

As for my name, growing up I always went by Randy, but even early on, when we were just dating, Kelley didn't think it fit me. She would always say, "You just don't sound like a Randy." She thought Randal was too formal and would simply call me Rand. I liked it. More important, Kelley liked it, and so it was pretty much settled. Aside from some of my old college friends who still tease me about the name change, no one really calls me Randy anymore. A lot of things changed when I met Kelley, the least of which was my name. Still, I've been Rand ever since.

When we met, my wife was living in Atlanta after having graduated from Rhodes College in Tennessee. I had spent four years at Duke University Medical School in Durham, North Carolina—Dad's alma mater—where I lived in the basement of a widow's house, mowed her grass in exchange for rent and would ride my bike to classes. After medical school, I spent a year and a half in Atlanta completing an internship in general surgery at Georgia Baptist Hospital. It was during that year that I met Kelley. We got married after I completed my general surgery internship in Atlanta, and Kelley moved to Durham, where I completed my ophthalmology residency. During that time we really liked North Carolina and thought we might stay there, and I was even close to signing a contract with a practice in a small town near Raleigh. We liked the beach, the mountains, the climate—it really suited us well. But when Kelley became pregnant with our first child she began to think about her home back in Kentucky, where her wonderful parents, Hilton and Lillian Ashby, grandparents and relatives all lived, and how important roots and community are when raising a family. Before becoming pregnant, Kelley had never wanted to move back home. But after a phone conversation with her mother one afternoon, I arrived home and Kelley said, "I've changed my mind." I was surprised at first, but immediately receptive. Kelley asked me to fly to Bowling Green, Kentucky to look into a particular practice her mother had mentioned. Two weeks later I did.

Without trying to sound too much like John Mellencamp, I grew up in a small town, always wanted to live in a small town and, of course, raise a family in a small town, and for eighteen of our twenty years of marriage Kelley and I have lived quietly in Bowling Green, Kentucky where we've raised our three boys, William, Duncan and Robert, and built my ophthalmology practice slowly, year after year, by persistence and word of mouth. I now have patients who come back to me because I had operated on their mother, grandfather or even great-grandfather and it is very gratifying and fulfilling. I chose the ophthalmology field because, as a teenager, I accompanied my grandmother on many trips to her eye surgeon. She underwent cataract surgery, corneal transplant surgery and ultimately laser treatment for macular degeneration. Because of this experience I wanted to become the kind of doctor who would help people see. Today, I have a picture of my grandmother in the foyer of my home in which she is sitting and eyeing the sights of her carbine with rifles in the background, something she did on occasion as a member of Ohio University's rifle team in the 1930s.

Kelley is originally from Russellville, Kentucky, about thirty miles south of Bowling Green. Her family, the Ashbys, have lived in Kentucky for generations. Some of Kelley's relatives served under Gen. George Washington during the American Revolution, and as payment for their service Capt. John Ashby received land in Lexington, Kentucky, and Capt. Stephen Ashby received land in Madisonville. You really can't get any more American or Kentukian than that. I mention this because during the general election my Democratic opponent tried to attack me for not being born in Kentucky. Using this logic, perhaps Reagan was not fit to serve as governor of California given that he was born in Illinois. Perhaps my father should not have been re-elected to Congress eleven times by his Texas constituents given that he was born in Pennsylvania. Perhaps Kelley's years spent in Tennessee and Atlanta, or my time in Texas, North Carolina and Atlanta somehow disqualify us both as "real" Kentuckians? When my primary opponent accused me of not being a Kentuckian I reminded voters that I have been a Kentuckian longer than he'd been a Republican. I've made my home in Kentucky for nearly two decades, where I've raised a family, started a medical practice, been involved in community organizations such as the Lions Club, founded the Southern Kentucky Lions Eye Clinic which provides eye exams and surgery to needy families and individuals, coached my three sons' little league baseball, soccer and basketball teams, and my wife is a deacon at the Presbyterian Church in Bowling Green to which we both belong. I don't think our American journey, personally, geographically or otherwise, is much different than that of most Americans. Kelley and I know where our home is and take great pride in where we've made it. This held true even as my Democratic opponent tried to insinuate otherwise, ironically enough in a desperate attempt to get to Washington, DC.

To my dismay and disgust, my Democratic opponent also tried to attack my Christian faith during the election by wildly misconstruing anonymous accusations about my college days that had made national headlines. I suppose if I had to run for the US Senate in Kentucky supporting President Obama's agenda, I might be inclined to pull out all the stops against my opponent as well. But to a man and a Christian, one can only stoop so low—even in the often nasty world of politics. Any electoral points that could've been gained would not have been worth the price—and for those who use such gutter politics, their tactics speak volumes about their character. The Bible says, "For what shall it profit a man, if he shall gain the whole world, and lose his own soul?" (Mark 8:36) I asked my Democratic opponent in one debate, "Have you no shame?

Have you no decency?" My Democratic opponent got what he deserved on November 2, 2010—and so did Kentucky.

Even during my medical studies, I've always remained politically minded and active, and one of the things I always liked about my days with Young Conservatives of Texas was how they rated the legislature on tax and spending issues and published the ratings. The group first did this as a gaggle of high school and college students and received statewide press for their ratings and I would replicate YCT's ratings example again and again. While completing my medical training, I founded and became chairman of the North Carolina Taxpayers Union, a watchdog group that scored politicians according to their tax and spending records. In a 1991 press release I stated,

> Taxpayers are sick and tired of being the scapegoat for irresponsible spending by politicians. As the budget deficit mushrooms, it's Joe Taxpayer who gets stuck with the bill. Politicians campaign "Read my lips, no new taxes," but reading between lips, we find that the politicians really meant "Yes, new taxes, many new taxes."

My distaste for the big government promoted by both parties—"read my lips, no new taxes" was George H.W. Bush's broken promise—has never wavered.

When I moved to Kentucky, Kelley and I and a handful of others started Kentucky Taxpayers United (KTU) in 1994 and published a "taxpayer scorecard" for over a decade. KTU also helped secure signed pledges from state legislators promising not to raise taxes. Part of KTU's mission statement in 1994 remains just as true today, not just for Kentucky but the entire country: "Every taxpayer in Kentucky knows well the limits of his or her own budget. The Kentucky legislature, however, seems to know no limits." At one point we had 55 legislators signed on to our no-new-taxes pledge. In our efforts to hold politicians' feet to the fire, predictably, Louisville's *Courier-Journal,* an unapologetically left-wing publication, would routinely criticize us for obstructing "progress"—by which they meant raising taxes. KTU's pledge influenced several races and we forced a number of politicians to sign it, which they did often out of embarrassment or for political expediency. Nevertheless, we forced them to be more transparent in their voting, which was the entire point. Many politicians would tout their KTU rating or the pledge in their ads and we raised substantial money to influence the political process toward objectives in line with our mission. Much like the Tea Party today, when KTU simply demanded accountability in government, we were portrayed as being part of the "party of no." Ultimately, our critics were right because if any entity needs to be obstructed or told "no" it's runaway government, whether at the state or federal level. Running up deficits and debt is not "progress." It's prolonged demise.

A Perfect Storm

As I've traveled Kentucky I've often noted that Thomas Jefferson wrote that each generation must renew its defense of liberty. I think each generation must renew and redefine what a political party stands for, remembering that political parties are but empty vessels unless we imbue them with values.

It must be stated time and again—having an "R" next to

our names means nothing unless we stand for something. In 1976, the battle was between the grassroots conservatives and the Eastern establishment as exemplified by Nelson Rockefeller. In 1964, it was the same battle between Barry Goldwater and the Eastern establishment. In the 2010 midterm elections the struggle was still the same, with the momentum that Reagan inspired in 1976 resurging in the form of the Tea Party to champion my campaign and others.

In the 2010 midterm election, it was unquestionably time for Tea. Mike Lee came from nowhere out of the ranks of the Tea Party to topple a sitting US Senator in the Republican primary. Lee's opponent, Sen. Bob Bennett, was targeted and defeated largely because he voted for the bank bailout. Lee went on to win the general election. After that, during the Kentucky GOP primary election, my Tea Party–endorsed campaign not only knocked off the establishment's pick, but did so handily, with my Republican opponent losing by a whopping 24 percent. There were Tea Party skirmishes in Nevada, Michigan, Colorado, Alaska and many other states throughout the country. Each candidate didn't win but, overall, the movement did. The media was unable to cover the elections without mentioning the ever-significant Tea Party factor. Status quo politicians scurried and the establishment was scared.

Clearly something big was happening.

People often ask me why I would go from a profession as a physician, one of the most respected, to one of the least respected as a politician. The answer is concern and worry. I, like other members of the Tea Party, became so concerned about the debt and what kind of a country we were passing on to our children and grandchildren that I felt that something must be done to reverse course. I felt the problem was even more imminent with the increasingly massive amounts of debt we were passing on and that the great recession and joblessness of 2009 and 2010 was directly related to this enormous burden of debt and economic uncertainty our leaders were creating.

I told my wife not to worry and that my chances of winning were probably less than 10 percent. After seeing how the establishment treated my father during his presidential campaign, I had every reason to believe that the powers-that-be would do everything they could to keep another Paul away from the reins of government. Besides, who would vote for a guy that would dare to tell voters the truth: not only did the emperor have no clothes, but the emperor also had no money. We were broke as a nation and our body politic was shattered. Certainly, it wasn't going to be fixed by the same old career politicians promising to bring home the bacon. It was going to take someone from the outside, a non-politician wielding a pickax—unafraid to use it.

As the campaign unfolded, Kelley told me that I would win. She says she knew it from the beginning, but I honestly did not. She worried how we would manage our family, the kids' school and the kids' sports. Being an eternal optimist, I promised that it would all work out. I always see the glass half full, and I have the same optimistic vision for our country if we can just get government out of the way.

Kelley always wanted me to wait—wait until we had the kids off to college, wait until we'd saved to pay for their tuition. Knowing my lifelong interest in politics, my obstetrician dad always told me he wished he had practiced medicine longer before getting into politics and that I shouldn't be in any hurry. My wife reminded me of Dad's advice. Kelley and I had always agreed that if I entered politics, it would be when we were older or at least in our fifties, something she mentioned when trying to talk me out of it. But I pointed out that we already were older and that our fifties weren't that far away. At first reluctantly, and then later enthusiastically, my wife eventually agreed with me. From the beginning, Kelley has always been my partner. This journey would be no different.

Overall, I knew that although no one individual typically creates current events, sometimes individuals can discern when current events create special opportunities. Sizing up the upcoming elections and unique political environment, I knew that my brand of constitutional conservatism might never find a better and more eager audience. The Tea Party, the mood of the country, and a president hell-bent on destroying business in America, combined to make 2010 the perfect storm—and the perfect constellation of events to elect an outsider with the zeal to reform, restrain and bind big government.

3

★ ★ ★

Equal Parts Chastisement, Republicans and Democrats

Members instinctively understand that the Republican brand is in the trash can. I've often observed that if we were a dog food, they would take us off the shelf.

–Rep. Tom Davis (R-VA), memorandum
to the Republican leadership,
May 14, 2008

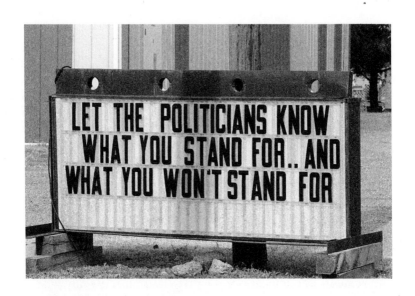

★ ★ ★

Imagine this—what if there had never been a President George W. Bush, and when Bill Clinton left office he was immediately replaced with Barack Obama. Now imagine Obama had governed from 2000 to 2008 exactly as Bush did—doubling the size of government, doubling the debt, expanding federal entitlements and education, starting the Iraq war—the whole works. To make matters worse, imagine that for a portion of that time, the Democrats actually controlled all three branches of government. Would Republicans have given Obama and his party a free pass in carrying out the exact same agenda as Bush? It's hard to imagine this being the case, given the grief Bill Clinton got from Republicans, even though his big government agenda was less ambitious than Bush's. Yet, the last Republican president got very little criticism from his own party for most of his tenure.

For conservatives, there was no excuse for this.

It seems some Republicans still haven't learned their lesson. Given the even worse excesses of the Obama administration, a Republican group erected a billboard last year featuring a smiling George W. Bush with the caption, "Miss me yet?" Any self-described conservative who "misses" the last president and his version of the Republican Party should probably quit subscribing to that label. Obama has proved far worse than Bush, no doubt, but this doesn't make Bush preferable, unless preference is dictated solely by party affiliation. If judgment is based on spending and the budget, then Bill Clinton should be considered preferable to Bush, given that he spent less money than his successor. Thinking that Bush is preferable might be ideologically or emotionally soothing for some, in the same way it makes some people feel good to root for their favorite sports team. But when it comes to politics, it's useless—and worse, it's a large part of the reason our government is in such sad shape.

This sort of partisan nonsense has long shielded big government Republicans from having to answer for their voting records and is precisely the sort of useless politics that so many Americans are sick of. Such partisanship is also precisely what the Tea Party now stands against, firmly and fully. The word "conservative" came to lose its meaning as Republicans doubled government and the debt under their own watch. The Democrats are now tripling both and must be stopped—but by a return to fiscal and constitutional sanity, not simply the same old, status quo insanity under the same old Republican brand.

Equal Parts Chastisement, Republican and Democrat

The largest events of the US Senate primary election were all Tea Parties. At one event in Louisville, for instance, we had over four thousand people. True to form, these gatherings sprang from nowhere and occurred spontaneously across America. The Tea Party was, and is, more complicated than the left-wing media will admit, and it is worth pointing out that while the movement is conservative, it is not partisan.

In fact, what connected me most to the Tea Party was my willingness to examine and criticize my own party. I repeated in speeches everywhere across the state that the Tea Party targets Republicans every bit as much as Democrats in both parties' failure to control the debt and balance the budget. I pulled no punches. I told them that the Republicans doubled the debt and Democrats were tripling the debt. I told them it didn't just start with President Obama, although he has greatly exacerbated the problem. I told them that the problem had been creeping up for a generation or more and that the debt was a product of long-term failure to obey the constitutional limits on government power.

What sealed the deal after months of visiting with the individual Tea Parties was this: When asked, "Will you stand up to fellow Republicans if they try to expand the debt?" my answer was an unequivocal "Yes," and the people believed me. They believed me because in every speech for a year, I spoke out and said that the GOP platform does not support bailing out failed businesses, much less owning them. I said that a vote for the bank bailout bill was wrong for many reasons, and particularly in the way it was passed—a thousand pages long, printed at midnight and passed by noon the next day. No one read the bill. There were even handwritten edits in the margin of the bill when it was passed. Like so much legislation in Washington, the bank bailout bill came out of the shadows and was passed in the midst of a government-created crisis, featuring clauses, new regulations and new powers for government, inserted into its crevices by anonymous clerks in the dead of night.

The bank bailout bill represented everything that was wrong with Washington. A crisis occurs. No one bothers to discover that maybe government played a role in the crisis. Hands are wrung and everyone says, "Hurry, we must act! We must do 'the people's' bidding!" My father, a Congressman, told me that he had banking lobbyists calling him and asking him about certain sections of the bill, and he said "What bill?" He didn't have a copy yet. They replied, "We do, would you like to see it?" You know government is out of control when lobbyists have the bills before members of Congress. Who is writing the bills, Congress or the lobbyists? This was similar to how the Republicans hastily pushed through the PATRIOT Act in the wake of 9/11, also using fear mongering and hyperbole. In 2001, Democratic Rep. Bobby Scott complained about the PATRIOT Act and the mad dash to enact it: "I think it is appropriate to comment on the process by which the bill is coming to us. This is not the bill that was reported and deliberated on in the Committee on the Judiciary. It came to us late on the floor. No one has really had an opportunity to look at the bill to see what is in it since we have been out of our offices." Democratic Rep. John Conyers questioned the integrity of the voting process, saying, "We are now debating at this hour of night, with only two copies of the bill that we are being asked to vote on available to members on this side of the aisle."

My dad pointed out that virtually everyone who voted for the PATRIOT Act had not even seen the final bill and, whether it's the PATRIOT Act or bank bailouts, Ron Paul has always been able to see through the scare tactics both parties use to push through more big government. Today the Tea Party is ready to cut through the bull and take on both parties. Their bipartisan criticism makes the movement not only

a good fit for my father, but such bipartisanship was a require-
ment for the Tea Party to support his son. And I wouldn't
have had it any other way.

A Republican Party Gone Crazy

The GOP likes to say that it has a big tent, that many are
welcome. Well this weekend at the District Republican
Convention the tent seemed more like a pup tent. Ron Paul
supporters were denied any speaking time... What is it that
so scares Republicans about Ron Paul? Could it be that
he has the courage to criticize Bush for adding more than
$2 trillion to the deficit? Could it be that Ron Paul scares
them because he actually votes against deficit spending,
even when it comes from a Republican administration?
Rand Paul to the Bowling Green *Daily News*,
April 29, 2008

Running for US Senate, the "experts" kept telling me to quit
criticizing the Republican party. "You can't get elected that
way," they said. I responded, "You know what? I'm not afraid
to lose." The results speak for themselves and the election
of 2010 shows that the voters were ready to hear the truth.
Besides, if anyone deserved to be criticized it was the Republican Party of the last decade.

The Republicans during the eight years of Bush were an
abysmal failure. The president ran on a platform of "compas-
sionate conservatism" only to double the size of government
and the national debt. In 1996, Republican presidential nominee Bob Dole was talking about abolishing the Department

of Education in his speeches and it was an established part of the GOP platform. A decade later, Bush doubled the size of the Department of Education with the No Child Left Behind Act in 2001. Republican House Leader John Boehner would call No Child his "proudest achievement." In 2007, the McClatchy news service reported: "George W. Bush, despite all his recent bravado about being an apostle of small government and budget-slashing, is the biggest spending president since Lyndon B. Johnson. In fact, he's arguably an even bigger spender than LBJ." No small part of this was Bush enacting Medicare Plan D, the largest entitlement expansion in nearly half a century. Of course, there were the bank bailouts, the $700 billion Troubled Assets Relief Program, and the Iraq war—the official estimate of which cost as much as Obamacare and the unofficial price tag will undoubtedly end up being much higher, just like Obamacare. Much of this was done early in Bush's presidency when the GOP controlled all three branches of the federal government. In assessing the Republicans' record under Bush, it's hard to imagine anyone still defending their spending as conservative, "compassionate" or otherwise.

The Tea Party's critics like to paint the movement as "extreme." But considering the damage and debt caused by the Republicans in the last decade, it was the GOP establishment that had gone crazy, completely abandoning its purported role as the party of smaller government. A $13 trillion debt ceiling was insane under the Republicans and the Democrats have gone even more insane by raising it to $14 trillion under Obama. *Chicago Tribune* columnist Steve Chapman had an interesting way of describing the dynamic of Tea Party candidates:

They didn't get nominated because they look and sound like the popular image of a savvy, experienced, well-informed, practical-minded U.S. senator. They got nominated because they don't. They are often accused of craziness—one MSNBC commentator said (Nevada's Sharron) Angle "sounds like a mental patient." But to the tea partiers, that's not a bug; it's a feature. If a $1.4 trillion federal budget deficit represents sanity, they would prefer a candidate who escaped from the psych ward.

It is the establishments of both parties that have gone crazy with their spending and it's the Tea Party now trying to find a way back to fiscal sanity. The choices offered might not always be perfect, or the candidates ideal, but to the extent that our politics is trending away from the status quo and toward more honesty and responsibility in government, the Tea Party will understandably and justifiably support outsider candidates, however unconventional they may be.

And besides, it was unqualified support for the "respectable" and "mainstream" Republican Party that allowed the GOP to do so much damage, giving Obama and the Democrats an even more solid statist foundation on which to build, or as *The Economist* noted in 2004:

(W)hat sort of conservative is Mr. Bush? Ever since Barry Goldwater's quixotic bid for the White House in 1964, American conservatism has been a small-government philosophy. Ronald Reagan regarded government as the problem rather than the solution, and therefore shrank social programmes. Newt Gingrich's troops assaulted not just Lyndon Johnson's Great Society but also a pillar of

FDR's New Deal, the welfare system. Mr. Bush's track-record has been very different. Whilst cutting taxes in a dramatic way that Mr. Reagan would surely have applauded, he has relentlessly expanded both the scale and scope of central government—in order to advance the conservative cause. Mr. Bush has tried to preside over the birth of a new political philosophy: big-government conservatism.

Big Government Conservatism?

A significant part of conservatives' confusion when Bush was in office was that many of his top Cabinet members and advisers were a particular type of conservative, defined as "neo-conservatives." Many have argued that this group isn't really conservative at all, but are simply confused as such due to their hawkish views and heavy involvement and influence within the Republican Party. Concerned first and foremost with projecting what they like to call "American power" around the globe through our military, this particular group has always been fairly comfortable with big government in contrast to traditional conservatives. Much of this comfort has to do with the fact that many neoconservatives migrated to the Republican Party from the Democratic Left in the late 1960s, 1970s and 1980s and also recognition that a global military presence necessarily requires a massive bureaucracy at home to support it. Many neoconservatives rejected Lyndon Johnson's Great Society, but would still argue the need for some sort of welfare state. Whereas traditional conservatives had once defined themselves by opposing Franklin Roosevelt and the

New Deal, neoconservatives were never as opposed to an energetic and interventionist state and typically considered FDR an exemplary president.

This group would have much influence in the Bush administration, with some neoconservatives even being openly enthusiastic about the prospect of finally wedding statism and conservatism together through the agenda of the new Republican president, or as columnist Fred Barnes explained in *The Wall Street Journal* in 2003:

> The case for Bush's conservatism is strong. Sure, some conservatives are upset because he has tolerated a surge in federal spending, downplayed swollen deficits, failed to use his veto, created a vast Department of Homeland Security, and fashioned an alliance of sorts with Teddy Kennedy on education and Medicare. But the real gripe is that Bush isn't their kind of conventional conservative. Rather, he's a big government conservative. This isn't a description he or other prominent conservatives willingly embrace. It makes them sound as if they aren't conservatives at all. But they are. They simply believe in using what would normally be seen as liberal means—activist government—for conservative ends. And they're willing to spend more and increase the size of government in the process.

"Big government conservative?" Willing to "spend more and increase the size of government in the process?" Who'd ever heard of such a thing? What kind of conservatism was this? To his credit, Barnes made clear that Bush's big government conservatism was a definite break from the traditional variety:

Conservative critics insist Bush is no Ronald Reagan—and they're right. Reagan was the leader of the conservative movement before he entered the White House. In his initial years as president, he cut taxes as boldly as Bush and curbed domestic spending. But Reagan was a small government conservative who declared in his inauguration address that government was the problem, not the solution. There, Bush begs to differ.

Former Reagan adviser Bruce Bartlett explains not only the absurdity of Barnes' narrative, but how conservatism properly understood has always been an outright rejection of what Bush represented:

The point is that George W. Bush has never demonstrated any interest in shrinking the size of government. And on many occasions, he has increased government significantly. Yet if there is anything that defines conservatism in America, it is hostility to government expansion. The idea of big government conservatism, a term often used to describe Bush's philosophy, is a contradiction in terms. Conservative intellectuals have known this for a long time, but looked the other way for various reasons. Some thought the war on terror trumped every other issue. If a few billion dollars had to be wasted to buy the votes needed to win the war, then so be it, many conservatives have argued. Others say that Bush never ran as a conservative in the first place, so there is no betrayal here, only a failure by conservatives to see what he has been all along.

A failure indeed. Whether out of party loyalty or delusions of grandeur, most Republican politicians and many GOP rank-and-file would blindly follow Bush's big government lead, and the neoconservatives' influence was most evident in the GOP's obsession with an aggressive foreign policy above all other principles, constitutional, conservative or otherwise.

During the 2008 Republican National Convention, my father—a strict, limited government, constitutional conservative—was denied a place at the convention, and ended up holding his own counter-convention across the street. But Sen. Joe Lieberman—a big government, socially liberal, former Democrat who had been Al Gore's running mate—was given a convention speaking role during prime time. Why? Despite his unimpeachable conservatism, my father had dared to question his own party on foreign policy and despite Lieberman's unabashed liberalism, he was an unwavering champion of that same policy. Little else seemed to matter to the Republican establishment at the time.

When during the 2008 presidential campaign John McCain was voting for TARP while also famously saying that America might stay in Iraq for "a hundred years," his actions and rhetoric reflected the exact same anti-conservative and war-crazy mentality that had dominated the Bush era. During the 2008 election the big government conservatives were still firmly in control of the Republican Party, and the GOP's presidential nominee was representative of that brand. Americans ended up rejecting that brand and embraced Obama.

Now the Tea Party rejects both brands.

Even Worse Than Bush

During the campaign, I came up with the idea of an old-fashioned, barnstorming bus tour that, interestingly enough, would happen to take place during the week of my boys' spring break. Given the hardships of a prior RV experience we'd had, my wife asked, "So now we're going across the state for eight full days, with three boys, in a bus?" I told her "yes" and promised we'd make it fun. We would let the boys play guitar on stage and, I reassured her, it would be a great experience for everyone. Of course I was not entirely convinced myself and after I saw the schedule, even less so. I had five to seven speeches and campaign stops per day, and while we would be staying in hotels each night, we had to be on the bus, ready to roll, each morning at seven o'clock. I should probably mention that my sons' ages are seventeen, fourteen, and eleven. Getting teenagers to wake up early on a weekend requires an act of Congress to begin with and we were asking them to commit to eight days of this during their spring break—while all of their friends were in Florida. William asked just one time if he could go with a friend's family to Florida, then never mentioned it again. He didn't complain, and we campaigned as a family. I thought the trip made sense because the concerns I had for my own family are what prompted me to enter the political arena to begin with. I really wanted to meet and connect with other Kentucky families to better understand their concerns.

And there were plenty of concerns—something our political and media elites still don't fully grasp or perhaps, as I've said before, don't care to.

When Barack Obama was elected president, he and his party assumed they had a mandate—a mandate for bigger government, more programs, and permission to run up greater debt. They were mistaken. The 2008 election reflected an America tired of Bush, but not necessarily in love with Obama, and it took only two years for the country to also sour on the Democrats, a message the administration heard loud and clear in the midterm election. To his credit, Senate Minority Leader Mitch McConnell seemed to get it and reminded everyone after the midterm elections that "voters didn't suddenly fall in love with Republicans; they fell out of love with Democrats." Republicans still jubilant over the midterm election and excited about their prospects in 2012 should remember and heed McConnell's words.

So should President Obama. If President Bush expanded government more than any president since LBJ, Obama has now expanded government even more than Bush. This is quite a feat and it makes Obama the most big government president in history already—with at least two years still left to go in his presidency. Contrary to his supporters' belief, Obama's agenda has not been a reversal of Bush's agenda but an extension of it, only more ambitious in its scope and even more reckless in spending. Amazingly, and perhaps ironically, even on the issues that once most animated the Left against the Republicans—prolonged war, civil liberties infringements, the further empowerment of the executive branch—Obama has basically maintained the same policies as his predecessor, and in some cases has expanded them. During the last presidential campaign Obama claimed that a vote for McCain was a vote for four more years of Bush. As it turns out, a vote for Obama was also a vote for four more years of Bush—crammed into two years and down the throats of American voters, whether they liked it or not.

In 2008, many Americans likely thought things couldn't get any worse than they were under Bush. They were wrong.

Today, after bank bailouts, auto bailouts, mortgage bailouts, stimulus, cap and trade, new bank regulations, new business regulations and, arguably, the worst part of the president's agenda in most Americans' minds—government-mandated healthcare—voters are genuinely concerned about the very future of their country. I don't think its hyperbole to say—and the most recent election supports this—that many Americans are genuinely afraid not only of what the Obama administration has done to date, but what it might do next.

And who can blame them? This concern is what I saw time and again out on the campaign trail. Speaking at a family-owned restaurant in Lexington, Kentucky, I asked a crowd of supporters, no doubt filled with Tea Partiers, "Does anyone think the president is taking us in the wrong direction?" The thunderous applause that followed is what some might dismiss as mere partisan cheerleading, and while such cheering is unquestionably part of any political campaign, Democrats might also want to remember that I won the election in a state in which approximately 60 percent of voters are registered with their party. But not surprisingly, my message—the Tea Party message—cut across party lines. I warned the audience that day:

We're in the midst of the worst recession since the Great Depression. If you ask people in business, "Is this worse than 1981 and '82?" Everyone that I've asked says that it's worse. We've had consistent unemployment that drags on and on. We're at 10 percent unemployment not counting those who've given up looking for work. In the midst of this recession the president has said we need more regulation and more taxes. That is exactly the wrong thing to do in a recession. With Obamacare we have the government overtaking one-sixth of the economy, but it's not just about the president getting in between you and your doctor and your ability to make decisions about healthcare, it's about new regulations, it's about increased premiums—my premiums have already gone up 15 percent—and it's about businesses having to pay fines in the middle of a recession. One businessman came up to me and said he will have to pay $400,000 in fines. These government programs will only create more debt. It's not like we have a bank where all this money is; what we have is a bank that's full of nothing. We have a bunch of paper that basically says we owe China $800 billion or Japan $700 billion. We won the Cold War but now owe the Russians $147 billion. The list goes on and on. We were once a great country in exporting and manufacturing items but now our number one export is our debt—and that's not a good thing to be exporting.

I would tell audiences these things not to frighten them but to be straight with them. Somebody had to. Of course, sometimes I didn't have to tell them—they already knew, or at least sensed, what was happening to their country and certainly knew a lot more than Obama and his party might give them credit for. But it was important that I let them know that I was on their side and wasn't just another opportunistic politician. Just because I was running under the Republican banner didn't necessarily mean I was the GOP's advocate, something they also knew instinctively and were suspicious about.

It was this healthy disgust at what the Republicans had done, combined with an acute awareness of what the Democrats were doing, that had created and defined the Tea Party.

To Seriously Oppose Big Government, There Must Be Serious Opposition

Democrats have never pretended to be champions of small government. Republicans have for decades. You really don't have an "opposition party" when that party has neither the intention nor the desire to truly oppose anything. When Sen. Jim DeMint said he'd rather have forty Republicans in the US Senate who were serious conservatives as opposed to a Republican majority that wasn't conservative, I understood exactly what he meant.

As bad as the Democrats are, I've focused on the Republican Party and its many shortfalls in this chapter, because in order to comprehensively stop Obama's agenda, the GOP is going to have to finally be dead serious about stopping it. Consider this—what kind of person would talk about how badly the neighbors' kids behave while ignoring the bad behavior of their own children? That person would seriously have their priorities out of whack, and it will continue to be of little use to conservatives for Republicans to bash Democrats for sport when they have no intention of doing any better. We desperately need a *real* "party of no." The Tea Party now demands it.

Throughout the campaign and my courtship with the Tea Party, I was not only reminded of earlier Tea Party events held in support of my father's presidential campaign, but how the 2008 Republican National Convention and Dad's counter-rally across the street represented the same contrast between the current GOP establishment and grassroots conservatives. Calling the counter-convention a "Rally for the Republic," everyone from conservative pundit Tucker Carlson, who was the rally's emcee, to my dad's old friend Barry Goldwater, Jr., spoke at the event. Speaker after speaker explained how the Republican Party and the mainstream conservative movement had gone awry. Over 10,000 tickets, symbolically priced at $17.76, were sold and the Founding Fathers' philosophy was alive and well on stage, in the crowd and in the organizer's statement that the rally was "a clear call to the Republican Party to return to its roots of limited government, personal responsibility, and protection of our natural rights."

Rally goers held many different signs but one of the most popular, and the slogan that stuck with me, read "Calling the GOP Back to Its Roots."

In spirit and in practice, this would also be my campaign slogan—as the Republican establishment was about to learn the hard way.

4

★ ★ ★

Taking on the Establishment

[Barry] Goldwater's politics were once considered the bedrock of American conservatism and yet today create so much controversy, not only for the Left...but for the mainstream Right which finds Rand's greatest vice to be his "extremist" brand of liberty, of which they can find no virtue. This ridiculous, two-party status quo restricts substantive debate, impedes real reform and begs for revolution. And whether the establishment likes it or not—Rand Paul just might give it to them.

Jack Hunter, *The American Conservative*,
May 21, 2010

I announced my candidacy for US Senate in the spring of 2009. Not since Ron Paul ran for Congress in 1996 had so many Republican-establishment luminaries opposed a candidate in a primary. House Speaker Newt Gingrich endorsed Dad's opponent. Then-Texas Governor George W. Bush and his father, former president George H.W. Bush, endorsed my father's opponent. Both US Senators from Texas endorsed the other guy and 150 congressmen contributed to the effort to keep my father off Capitol Hill.

It was the second time Dad had run for Congress, and he re-entered politics after a twelve-year hiatus spent practicing medicine in Lake Jackson. Dad believed that the Republican Revolution of 1994 might have created a more receptive political environment for his constitutional, limited government message. My father wasn't completely alone in his campaign, as he raised funds through a network of dedicated conservatives and libertarians from all over the country. He was also helped by endorsements from tax activist Steve Forbes and then-Republican presidential candidate Pat Buchanan, who had been recently dubbed a "Hell Raiser" within the GOP on the cover of *Time*.

In 2010, the week before the general election, I appeared on the cover of *Time* as a "Party Crasher" in a story about how the insurgent Tea Party movement had defined the midterm elections. It was an apt description. Senate minority leader Mitch McConnell had endorsed my opponent in the primary, and so did former vice president Dick Cheney. Republican Sen. Rick Santorum endorsed the other guy along with former presidential candidate and New York City mayor Rudy Giuliani. The Republican establishment, both at the national level and in Kentucky, came out strong in trying to keep the son of Ron Paul from getting anywhere near Capitol Hill too.

Like Dad, I was inspired by the current political environment to explore whether or not my constitutional, limited government message might have a significant audience. Also, like Dad, I wasn't completely alone. I had an army of dedicated conservatives and libertarians who were generous in funding my campaign, many of whom had also supported my father's presidential run in 2008. I received the endorsement of former Alaska governor Sarah Palin and Sen. Jim DeMint, both heroes to conservatives for taking on the party establishment. I also received the endorsement of Christian leader James Dobson and, not surprisingly, Steve Forbes. Also not surprisingly, pundit and renegade Republican Pat Buchanan had many kind words for my campaign throughout the election.

Against all odds, my father won his 1996 bid for Congress and has been "raising hell" on Capitol Hill ever since. In 2010, I would do the same—the party establishment be damned.

Cracks in the Establishment Game Plan

In the fall of 2008, the GOP got the first indication that I might run for Senate. I sent a letter to all the Republican county chairs expressing my frustration with the party, but at the time I honestly wasn't certain I would run, both unsure if the political environment was ripe enough or if events would unfold in a way that might present the opportunity. My congressman was new and conservative, only forty-five years old, and could well be in Congress for twenty or thirty years. My letter was a two page critique in which I let the county parties know that I was annoyed with the bank bailout, and I got some flak for my letter being "anti-Republican" due to my harsh criticism of the GOP's culpability in the matter. Regardless, I felt it was important to express these concerns to fellow Republicans, and hoped I could do so at some upcoming meetings. However, I sent out sixty letters and received almost no responses—with the exception of overwhelmingly negative feedback.

I did get two offers: one from the Logan County Republican Party, the county where my wife grew up and her parents reside, and I was invited to speak at their annual Lincoln Day Dinner. The second was from the Carroll County GOP to speak at their next scheduled meeting. This offer came a good while after I had sent the letter, and after driving three hours to speak, there were only five people at the forum.

There had been rumors and rumblings for a while that Kentucky's junior US Senator, Jim Bunning, was being forced out by the state's senior senator, Mitch McConnell. Not long after I had sent out my letter raising a minor stink within the state party, Bunning decided not to seek a third term. Never one to mince words, Bunning was blunt about his reasons: "Over the past year, some of the leaders of the Republican Party in the Senate have done everything in their power to dry up my fundraising. The simple fact is that I have not raised the funds necessary to run an effective campaign for the U.S. Senate."

Time reported on Bunning's announcement: "The notoriously irascible and unpredictable Bunning finally bowed to the one immutable reality of Kentucky politics: Republicans can't win without the support of Mitch McConnell."

Not long after, and because of, Bunning's announcement, I decided to run. And thanks to the Tea Party, this supposedly "immutable reality" of Kentucky politics would soon be muted.

Senator Bunning (the senator was also a professional baseball legend), appeared and spoke at the "Old Fifth" Lincoln Day Dinner with about five hundred in attendance. ("Old Fifth" was the nickname given to the western half of Kentucky's 5th congressional district, which has been solidly Republican for generations.) That night Bunning was inducted into the Kentucky GOP Club's Hall of Fame, and he warned the audience about Obama, expressed his concerns about national security, but also remarked, "I've been booed by sixty thousand fans at Yankee Stadium, so I don't get rattled when thirty-nine other senators think I voted the wrong way." He gestured toward McConnell, who sat nearby.

On the way out, I positioned myself to exit through the same door as Senator Bunning just to say hello and, for the first time, he acknowledged my name and said to call him. This was a far cry from our first meeting on the campaign trail the previous summer when he completely spurned me and, as I recall, really just turned away from me when I introduced myself. That day his wife was more engaging and we talked about a nice lunch she'd had with my mother, which Mom remembered fondly, a few years before.

When I called Senator Bunning, he told me that the GOP establishment were going to paint me as a radical. He said he'd heard them talking among themselves at a recent dinner, adding, "but I have big ears." Bunning said the GOP establishment controlled all the money interests and Grayson had all the big money in northern Kentucky. He went on to say that the GOP establishment was behind Dick Cheney's endorsement of Grayson and he thought they'd soon have more. He asked if I had DeMint coming in to Kentucky to give his endorsement, adding, "If push comes to shove, I want you to win." Those ten words were music to my ears. If Senator Bunning publicly endorsed me, it could put us over the top. We were surging, but this would be enormous. Despite what the media reported, Senator Bunning was still much loved, especially by Republicans, and most especially by Republicans in his old Congressional District of Northern Kentucky. We spoke for several minutes about the Federal Reserve, the destructive policies of which my father had been trying to rein in his entire career, and had been more successful than ever in getting bipartisan support to do just that in 2009. Bunning mentioned that he introduced legislation in 1987 to audit the Federal Reserve.

I had always admired Bunning's leadership and take-no-prisoners style, but my admiration grew even more when he single-handedly stood up against an unfunded Senate action that would end up being arguably the most controversial stand of his career—blocking the extension of unemployment benefits. The Senate had passed a "pay-as-you-go" rule, and Bunning had a problem with his colleagues simply still "going" along with their usual agenda without any idea of how to "pay" for it. Bunning wanted to make a point that when the Senate passes rules it should follow them. His fellow senators pleaded for Bunning to join them in a unanimous consent vote, but Bunning steadfastly refused. When Sen. Jeff Merkley (D-Ore.) begged him to change his mind, Bunning said, right there on the Senate floor, "Tough s***." Never one to shy away from a good fight, Bunning's stance was never a matter of wanting to deny unemployment benefits; he simply didn't believe we should be adding to the deficit. Where else could we possibly cut spending to pay for these extensions? It was a perfectly reasonable question, even though the senator was continually attacked by completely unreasonable people.

There was no question that Bunning was upset with the Republican leadership over the way he'd been treated, but also, quite legitimately, with that same leadership's carefree attitude toward spending and debt. Bunning's disgust with his party and politics in general reflected my own feelings expressed earlier in my letter to the state GOP. I would later tell a reporter, "I got started in this race actually to defend Jim Bunning against attacks...the one thing I really admired about him was that he wasn't afraid to stand on principle. He stood up and, on principle, voted the way he believed was right for Kentucky and I'm proud of him for that." I wasn't the only conservative who would champion Bunning's stance and it coincided perfectly with not only the evolution of the Tea Party but my insurgent campaign. During the tumultuous primary, Bunning would endorse me, something the media considered a dig at the Republican leadership as much as a vote of confidence in me.

Crashing the Party

The tea party movement may well be the most powerful and potent force in America.
                    Scott Rasmussen and Douglas E. Schoen,
                            Politico.com

The man who was supposed to become Kentucky's next US Senator was Trey Grayson—Kentucky's secretary of state, former Democrat-turned-Republican, and McConnell's hand-picked replacement for Bunning. As Jim Bunning noted, Grayson was being privately supported behind the scenes by the GOP establishment, both in Kentucky and nationally. When I announced my candidacy I was at 15 percent in the polls and, as I've mentioned, couldn't even get invited to any Republican forums—but I was getting invited to Tea Party forums. That movement would end up being the life of the party, both figuratively and literally, as the old Republican guard had nothing to offer—and some of its most distinguished guardsmen would not be able to stop the Tea Party tidal wave that would eventually define the entire race.

McConnell would end up endorsing Grayson in the eleventh hour, but before that the Republican establishment would bring out many big guns in conjunction with my increasing poll numbers, and they would also try to use the same tactics they used against my father when he ran for president in 2008. When the old guard went after my dad, they lit a fire under thousands if not millions of liberty-minded Americans who would embrace my father's limited government message, rallying enthusiastically around his campaign and staunchly against the establishment. Dad wouldn't get the nomination but he would do something no other presidential candidate would—create a "Ron Paul Revolution" that would help form and inspire the Tea Party, break fundraising records, influence a new generation of conservatives, take Dad's popularity to new heights—and help fund my campaign. Sure, McCain won the nomination in 2008—but alas, there was no "John McCain Revolution."

Nor was there a "Rudy Giuliani Revolution." Giuliani had done a superb job of handling 9/11 and had hoped to parlay that popularity into a GOP presidential nomination in 2008. Giuliani was considered an early frontrunner by many analysts but ended up receiving even fewer delegates than my father. Nevertheless, Giuliani remains a well-known name within the party. The Republican establishment thought Giuliani endorsing my opponent might boost Grayson's credibility and help counter my increasing poll numbers, but it didn't. Even less effective were Giuliani's attacks on me, which were pretty much the same tactics he tried to use on my father during the presidential debates, insinuating that somehow Dad "blamed" America for 9/11. Wrote *Reason* magazine's James Antle after the endorsement:

If former New York City Mayor Rudy Giuliani has anything to say about it, the political sins of the father will be visited on the son. On Patriots Day, Giuliani endorsed Trey Grayson in the Republican primary race for U.S. Senate in Kentucky. But the endorsement had as much to do with GOP frontrunner Rand Paul—and his father, Rep. Ron Paul (R-Texas)—as it did Grayson. "Trey Grayson is the candidate in this race who will make the right decisions necessary to keep America safe and prevent more attacks on our homeland," Giuliani said in a statement. "He is not part of the 'blame America first' crowd that wants to bestow the rights of U.S. citizens on terrorists and point fingers at America for somehow causing 9/11." Other prominent hawks have since joined Giuliani in this line of attack.

"Prominent hawks," indeed. Besides mischaracterizing my actual positions concerning how to handle terror suspects, among other things—as he once mischaracterized my father's positions on virtually everything—Giuliani was the sort of socially liberal, moderate Republican who had become popular with the GOP establishment because, for them, having hawkish views trumped everything else. Once again, this has always been characteristic of the neoconservatives. Neither my father nor I have ever "blamed America" for Islamic terrorism, though we do blame Giuliani for continuing to spin this absurd narrative every time an establishment candidate finds himself challenged by someone with the last name Paul.

Next came Dick Cheney, who was even worse than Giuliani. Arguably no GOP figure represented the sort of big government Republicanism the Tea Party was explicitly rejecting more than the former vice president. When Bush was spending at breakneck speed, Cheney famously shot back at critics that "deficits don't matter" and apparently thought they still didn't matter in my race against Grayson. But what issues did matter to Cheney? Echoing Giuliani, Cheney stated his belief that I was somehow deficient on the singular issue that had defined *his* Republican Party, saying in his endorsement of my opponent: "Trey Grayson is right on the issues that matter—both on fiscal responsibility and on national security." Fiscal responsibility? Was the vice president really going there? Did they somehow believe I wasn't fiscally conservative enough? But everyone knew what they meant: They were questioning my conservative credentials because they didn't believe I was "hawkish" enough. I had stated repeatedly throughout the campaign that the primary role of the federal government is national security, and the accusations against me from neo-conservatives were beginning to become a parody. *Reason's* Antle explained well what "issue" truly "mattered" most to Cheney and his establishment friends: " 'I'm a lifelong conservative, and I can tell the real thing when I see it,' Cheney said in his endorsement of Grayson, pronouncing the candidate 'right on the issues that matter.' As with Giuliani, it was clear that the issue that mattered was Rand Paul and his father."

Cheney would inject himself into just a few races in the mid-term election, and almost all of those candidates would lose.

So, to a significant degree, would the Republican establishment.

A Letter to Sarah

In contrast to Grayson's top-down Republican machine, much of my momentum came from the bottom up, reflecting the grassroots nature of the Tea Party and my campaign. While my opponent and his advisers were trying to scare voters by portraying me in a negative light, my campaign became a steamroller of positive energy, gathering steam at each stop and more adherents with each speech. It was truly fulfilling to see my message, which a few short months ago couldn't get a hearing at local Republican forums, finding an excited and growing audience at Tea Parties all over Kentucky.

Some of those supporters came early and, in some ways, were the most amazing. Take, for example, Larry Hodge of Grayson County, Kentucky. Larry is a longtime Republican activist, Church of Christ minister, father of two and grandfather of five. Larry dropped by my medical office when we were brainstorming one day and said he'd like to help, asking what we needed. He overheard us talking about how "our people" were trying to communicate with "Sarah Palin's people." We had been sending Palin's camp information for the past few months trying, unsuccessfully to date, to win her endorsement.

Larry said he'd take care of this for us. My first thought was, *Sure he will.* I couldn't help but be a bit doubtful that he would waltz right in from Grayson County and secure us Sarah Palin's endorsement. But Larry would go home and begin writing a heart-to-heart, Christian-to-Christian letter, telling Palin that there was a "true Republican" and "real conservative" running for the US Senate in Kentucky, and asked if she would consider endorsing me, or at least pray over it and give it some thought. Larry then went online, looked up Palin's mailing address and sent the letter off to Wasilla, Alaska.

It didn't take long to get a response. When Larry called us and said Palin's people would be calling with an endorsement, our jaws dropped. I asked, "How in the world did you accomplish this?" He said, "Well, I just sent her a registered letter to her house in Wasilla, Alaska, and they called me a few days later."

And that's how I received Sarah Palin's endorsement.

That Palin would take the time to read and consider a fan letter (she must receive tons) was just another example of her genuine and personal concern for her fellow countrymen and, as a conservative who had taken on the GOP establishment in her own state as governor of Alaska, Palin was an ideal fellow traveler for our campaign. Said Palin in her endorsement:

I'm proud to support great grassroots candidates like Dr. Paul. While there are issues we disagree on, he and

I are both in agreement that it's time to shake up the status quo in Washington and stand up for common sense ideas.

Palin's endorsement gave us a boost that energized supporters, brought in new ones and, of course, annoyed my opponent and his Republican bosses to no end.

Palin called the house on a Saturday morning. It was impossible not to recognize that distinctive Alaskan accent. She wanted to know my position on Israel. I said that Israel was an important ally, the only democracy in the Middle East and that I would not vote to condemn Israel for defending herself. Later, after Palin's endorsement of me, she was grilled about it by FOX News' Chris Wallace. Of course, she defended it. William Kristol, FOX contributor and editor of the neoconservative *Weekly Standard,* would reply, "I'm disappointed by her endorsement of Paul. . . . But they always disappoint you."

In talking to Palin, one of the primary things I wanted to do was allay any fears about social issues, telling her, "My opponents call me a libertarian but I want to assure you that I am pro-life." Palin responded, "Oh, we all have a little libertarian in us."

I do not apologize for believing there is too much government involvement in the private lives of Americans. Trying to portray me or my father as not pro-life—or saying I want to legalize heroin, or prostitution or making other outlandish claims—are smears Republican establishment types have always attempted. This race would be no different. One could make the argument that if sincerity is measured by proposed legislation, my dad is arguably the most pro-life member of the House.

As the primary season accelerated, the attacks intensified and my opponent put out literature and phone calls claiming I wasn't pro-life. For a brief moment, it worked. Focus on the Family founder Dr. James Dobson is one of the nation's most respected Christian leaders and he had initially endorsed Grayson. The next day I spoke at a pro-life rally in Paris, Kentucky, where a gentleman came up to me after my speech and told me he was an OB/GYN from Lexington, Dr. Lewis Hicks. We began talking, and when he asked about Dobson's endorsement, I admitted my disappointment. Dr. Hicks said he liked my speech, believed I was sincere and said he'd see what he could do. Hicks was fairly confident, saying "I know Dr. Dobson. I'll call him and take care of this." Like Larry Hodge, I was doubtful of what kind of results Dr. Hicks would get but appreciated his concern and effort. And like Hodge, Dr. Hicks was yet another example of the many everyday Kentuckians who would rally to my campaign and against the Republican establishment, sometimes significantly altering the course of events to my advantage.

The next morning Dr. Hicks called and said, "Dr. Dobson would like to speak with you. He's reconsidering his endorsement." I was silent. I really didn't quite believe what I was hearing. Dr. Hicks continued, "Dr. Dobson wants you to call him." I asked, still stunned, "Are you sure? I hate to bother him if he's already decided." Later that day I spoke with Dr. Dobson for about fifteen to twenty minutes. I'll never forget him saying, "I haven't been to one of these Tea Parties yet, but I think I'd probably fit right in."

Dobson switched his endorsement and we ran radio commercials across the state. After that, it was impossible for anyone to question my pro-life credentials and in his endorsement statement, Dobson was clear about the fact that he had pretty much been lied to and who, exactly, had changed his mind, saying, "Senior members of the GOP told me Dr. Paul is pro-choice and that he opposes many conservative perspectives, so I endorsed his opponent. But now I've received further information from OB/GYNs in Kentucky whom I trust, and from interviewing the candidate himself."

The momentum was gathering and with it would come more endorsements, both to help and hurt my campaign.

"The Issues That Matter"

I rarely endorse in primaries, but these are critical times.
Sen. Mitch McConnell

McConnell's endorsement of Grayson was indeed a rare move by a man in his position, but, as he noted, it was a critical time—it looked like his handpicked candidate was about to suffer a major defeat. When McConnell was putting in a last-ditch effort to save Grayson's campaign, I was ahead in the polls by a large margin and was being discussed as the first possible major victory for the Tea Party. It was an exciting time for me and the movement.

McConnell's endorsement also led to another big one for my campaign—Sen. Jim DeMint. Like Palin, DeMint had been called a Tea Party "kingmaker," and while my standing with the Tea Party was already solid, DeMint was one of the senators I was looking forward to working with most. DeMint had been a supporter both ideologically and financially, but had held off his endorsement until McConnell, who he obviously had to work with, decided to enter the fray.

I was glad to have him. In my fight for fiscal conservatism I would likely not have a better ally in the Senate than DeMint. When my father was gathering support for legislation to audit the Federal Reserve in the House, it was DeMint, along with Sen. Bernie Sanders, who cosponsored the sister legislation in the Senate. DeMint had made a name for himself in taking on the establishment and shared my belief that massive debt would lead to America's downfall. In his book *Saving Freedom*, DeMint warned that "our greatest enemy is not a foreign government or even a terrorist group," but big government. This was *the* issue, without question, or as DeMint stated in his endorsement: "Rand Paul is a true conservative who will stand up to the Washington establishment. He has been running on the issues that matter since the beginning of this campaign." The neocons said I was lacking on the "issues that matter." Their comments were almost laughable considering their utter disregard for the national debt. DeMint disagreed, adding, "[Rand Paul] is a strong advocate for balanced budgets, he wants to end the culture of earmarks, he supports term limits, and he's 100 percent pro-life. He's not a career politician and he's got the guts to stand up to the massive spending, bailouts, and debt that are being forced on us in Washington."

When tax activist Steve Forbes endorsed me, he expressed the same fiscal concerns as DeMint: "I see in Rand someone who can take the fight from the Tea Parties to the Senate, and help take back our government and our country from the out-of-control, tax-and-spend liberals. Rand Paul will do the work to fight for lower taxes and spending and for more freedom in Washington. He'll fight for a constitutional amendment to balance the budget and for term limits. He'll fight to give back more of our rights, not take more away. I can't think of a better way to represent the people of Kentucky than to end the cycle of career politicians and pork barrel spending in Washington."

The issue that mattered most was big government, and though Grayson wasn't in Washington, DC when Bush-era Republicans were doing so much damage, he was perceived as a representative of that brand. And no matter who Grayson's camp brought out to attack me—Giuliani, Cheney, former senator Rick Santorum, Rep. Hal Rogers—the staleness of the old Republican guard simply would not overpower the aroma of Tea.

McConnell Agrees to Meet

Senator McConnell would campaign hard against me for the obvious reasons, but above all the senator was pragmatic.

My staff eventually called Senator McConnell's people to arrange a meeting. Unlike every other candidate running for any position in Kentucky, I did not call him in advance to tell him I would be running for office, only after I had been running for several months and the polls showed us within striking distance or possibly ahead. While our meeting was intended to extend an olive branch to McConnell, many on his side still felt it insulting that we had not called earlier to "ask for permission." In fact, one of our first press releases of the campaign had read: "Many politicians go on bended knee to ask for permission to run for office. Rand Paul will be at Teresa's Diner to talk to Kentuckians about whether to run for office."

I was actually surprised that McConnell agreed to meet with me. He was already actively raising money for Grayson.

Through arm-twisting, the GOP establishment had influenced twenty-three US Senators (seventeen of whom had voted for the bank bailout) to sign on to a fundraiser for Grayson at the National Republican Senatorial Committee. Our grassroots supporters dubbed it the "bailout ball" and set up an online fundraising event for me they dubbed "a cage fight," complete with photo-shopped images of Grayson and myself. We raised $190,000 which probably exceeded Grayson's bailout ball, though they never released anything about their event.

My meeting with McConnell took place in a hangar at Bowman Field airport outside of Louisville, with Secret Service surrounding us. McConnell began the meeting cordially but quickly got to the point: "It looks like you're trying to run against me."

I tried to assure him that I wasn't running against him. He responded: "And what's this about opposing me for leadership?" I laughed and explained to the senator that I'd spent fifteen minutes avoiding a reporter who was trying to lead me into saying something negative about him, how all of my supporters who watched the interview were pleased that I had deflected the reporter's questions and had avoided getting involved in any name-calling. I told McComell that if you read the entire interview, I never once criticized the Senator and that the headline they ran—"Paul refuses to endorse McConnell for leadership"—was not only inaccurate, but we featured it on our website under the title "Paul compliments McConnell."

I reiterated my long-held support for McConnell in his court challenge to so-called "campaign finance reform" popularly known as McCain/Feingold. I told him that recently a student had asked if my support of term limits meant I was opposed to McConnell. I replied that, no, my support of term limits would mean that even my father would have to come home and that I wasn't running against my father either. McConnell responded that he didn't care what I did on term limits.

I tried to keep the conversation light. I remarked that when Grayson said I wasn't a Kentuckian, I'd had fun responding that I'd been a Kentuckian longer than he'd been a Republican, and besides, we have a very famous US Senator who was born in Alabama (McConnell smiled, knowing I was referring to his not being born in Kentucky). I tried to let him know I wasn't the enemy and that I would work together with him and the party. I told him what I told everyone. After the primary he would be the first person I called to ask for help. To his credit, he answered that call and became one of my biggest supporters in the general election. In fact, a month before the election he called for a unity rally three days after the primary. Republicans, with Senator McConnell's leadership, came out of the primary more united than the Democrats, who also had a contentious primary.

As our meeting continued, Senator McConnell reiterated that he didn't want to get involved in the primary. I thought to myself, "Not get involved—I wonder what it would mean if he *did* get involved."

Regardless, I left pleased that he agreed to meet with us. Of course the press got wind of it, and there was a statewide story saying a meeting was anticipated and another saying the meeting had already taken place. I felt that we got some positive media attention; and to many, that we'd held a meeting with McConnell meant we had become a force to be reckoned with. Some interpreted the meeting to mean that McConnell was beginning to hedge his bets—that the establishment now believed we could win.

A few of our more libertarian-minded supporters became angry at us for meeting with McConnell, interpreting it as "selling out to the establishment." An article appeared in the *Louisville Courier-Journal* about a staffer quitting because I had "forbidden" any criticism of McConnell. Inadvertently, this episode helped us with many mainstream Republicans who did not want to see another episode of squabbling among fellow Republicans.

The McConnell meeting was just the latest event among many indicating that the tide had turned almost entirely our way. The primary election was near—and it would be a tidal wave.

Randslide

I hold it that a little rebellion now and then is a good thing, and as necessary in the political world as storms in the physical.

Thomas Jefferson

On the morning of the primary election, May 18, 2010, satellite television trucks began rolling into Bowling Green. By afternoon, there were a dozen trucks, about a hundred production crew members and news anchors scattered all over the lawn of the Bowling Green Country Club. I think the magnitude of what was happening really began to sink in when

Kelley and I arrived at Briarwood Elementary School to cast our votes that morning. A throng of cameramen and reporters rushed our car as we pulled into the parking lot, already jam-packed with satellite television trucks. That morning, none of the reporters asked anything—everyone knew why we were there—and they just walked in front of and around us as we entered the school. It was a bit unnerving to my wife, but when a small group of poll workers applauded us as we walked in, it lightened the mood.

Walking out of the school, Kelley and I could see our sons were across the street waving signs along with friends and family, cheering us. All of my immediate family flew in from Texas for the night and my parents arrived around noon. We had planned a cookout on our back deck and prepared to settle in for a long night as election returns rolled in. Gathered at the house, we had a great dinner with our parents, my brothers and sisters and some close friends as we prepared for the returns. Our sons kept a close eye on their computers and the televisions, and Duncan kept running out to the deck with updates. I was prepared for at least another hour of waiting for returns, when suddenly there was an eruption in the living room and Duncan and Robert burst onto the deck shouting, "We won! We won! They called it! We won!"

The polls closed at 6 PM and by 7:30 PM the networks were calling the race. We won—big—with a 24-point spread. FOX News' Sean Hannity was calling it a "Randslide." The entire political world was shocked. In winning Kentucky's Republican Party primary for the US Senate, I was being declared as the first Tea Party candidate to actually win a statewide race.

Mom and Dad were beaming and hugged me. My sister Lori had tears streaming down her face and the kids were jumping around. All was a happy chaos, a chord of joy that ran through all of us at once. Kelley threw herself at me and we hugged in the middle of it all, everyone still whooping around us. It was a moment to behold and cherish—but not for long. As soon as we learned that we won, we were being rushed out the door—everyone wanted us at the victory party ASAP.

Of course, we didn't expect the returns to be in so soon, and our sons were still wearing T-shirts and basketball shorts, and even Kelley was still in jeans. We rushed the boys upstairs—pleading with them to put on the clothes Kelley had laid out for them, with my wife adding that please, for once, don't argue. William was angling for jeans and a golf shirt, Duncan was yelling that his clothes didn't fit, and Kelley rushed into the room to find his younger brother's carefully ironed shirt and khakis in a crumpled ball on the floor. Laughing, she told him, "Those are Robert's clothes, you goof!" In his excitement our fourteen-year-old son had tried to force himself into the pants of his eleven-year-old brother.

We pulled up to the portico at Bowling Green Country Club as a crowd of supporters and friends cheered and we were ushered through kitchens and around back so we could make our entrance. As we walked around to the back of the stage, I asked my boys, "I wonder where my song is?" Suddenly, the heavy drumbeat of "TNT" by AC/DC blasted into the night and my boys started laughing as I pumped my fist in the air to the beat. The mood, the music, the noise of the crowd, the hot lights hitting us as we stepped onstage, it was all a jolt of pure adrenaline—and it was unbelievable!

Conventional wisdom said it could not be done. Conventional wisdom said a guy who had never run for office and who opposed the concept of the federal government as an unlimited ATM could never win a statewide election. Conventional wisdom said that in order to win you must be Santa Claus and simply bring federal goodies to your constituents. Conventional wisdom said that you could not win if you told people the truth—admitting to voters that the pig had been picked clean, and that bringing home the bacon really meant borrowing from China and Japan to mortgage our children's future.

Conventional wisdom could have never predicted we would win by such a large margin, considering that over one hundred elected state officials endorsed the other guy, a significant number of Republican county chairmen would not even invite us to their forums and some of the most powerful leaders in the national GOP would come out against me, including Kentucky's senior senator.

So much for conventional wisdom.

5

★ ★ ★

Ready for Prime Time?

Fame is a bee
It has a song
It has a sting
Ah, too, it has a wing

Emily Dickinson

* * *

I always thought it couldn't be so bad to be famous. Movie stars and celebrities always carp about the media's lack of ethics, cameras being stuck in their faces and other intrusive tactics, crying about it as they cash their multimillion-dollar checks and vacation on the Riviera. I was about to discover that fame is not all it's cracked up to be, especially for an aspiring US Senator. I was also about to discover the sting of fame, but unlike a movie star, I would get no solace in any multimillion-dollar checks.

Three days after my primary victory, Kelley gave me the poem by Emily Dickinson that I use in the opening of this chapter. It was apropos. Winning one of the most high-profile primary races in the country had brought newfound celebrity, and with it heightened criticism that would veer into the absurd as the establishment did its best to discredit me and the Tea Party. Luckily, we prevailed—but it became very clear early on that I would be held to a different standard in a concerted effort to undermine the movement.

Attack of the Mainstream Media

The morning after my primary victory, I was up extra early for interviews.

Naturally, we expected the media requests would be heavy and there were still plenty of news crews coming into our neighborhood looking to get any coverage they could. What we thought was going to be a long day ended up being a long couple of days—and certainly longer than any of us could have anticipated.

The left-wing media wants so badly to paint the Tea Party as "extreme" or "racist" to both discredit it and to avoid having to discuss what the movement actually stands for. Some were caught in the act last year when a group of liberal reporters and bloggers who posted in a Google Groups forum called "Journolist" chatted openly online about how to defeat conservatives. When Jeremiah Wright's anti-American rhetoric became known, those liberal reporters plotted a way to shift the debate away from him, or as the *Washington Independent*'s Spencer Ackerman wrote on Journolist in 2008, "If the right forces us all to either defend Wright or tear him down, no matter what we choose, we lose the game they've put upon us. Instead, take one of them—Fred Barnes, Karl Rove, who cares—and call them racists."

Of course, most conservatives are all too familiar with this common tactic used by the Left against the Right, but to come out and say it openly was quite amazing. Ackerman continued with his instructions on how to take down conservatives: "Ask: why do they have such a deep-seated problem with a black politician who unites the country? What lurks behind those problems? This makes 'them' sputter with rage, which in turn leads to overreaction and self-destruction." Ann Coulter responded to Ackerman's comments: "This is what 'racism' has come to in America. Democrats are in trouble, so they say 'let's call conservatives racists.' We always knew it, but the Journolist postings gave us the smoking gun." Added Coulter: "This explains why we've heard so much about Tea Partiers being 'racists' lately."

At the height of our primary victory and within the first twenty-four hours, I would learn firsthand about this tactic.

On election night, the television trucks lined up and the next morning every national news show in the country requested an appearance. We rented our own satellite truck to accommodate back-to-back-to-back morning talk shows. I got up at 4 AM and began doing shows at 5 AM. I did fourteen national interviews before 8 PM that evening, when my final interview of the day was scheduled with MSNBC's Rachel Maddow. I had already heard fame's song—but not yet felt its sting.

In the early afternoon Kelley called to say that my Democratic opponent, Jack Conway, had gone on MSNBC and said I was for the repeal of the Civil Rights Act—a position I had never taken. My wife said she was just flipping through the news channels but had stopped when she saw Conway on Chris Matthews' *Hardball*. She was shocked to hear my opponent say that I had called for repeal of the 1964 Civil Rights Act during my interview with the editorial board of the Louisville *Courier-Journal*. Kelley said she began to feel ill watching Conway try to portray me as some kind of racist. Angry and bewildered, my wife had even pulled up my interview with the newspaper online to see exactly what these men were talking about. After all, I had given countless interviews at this point. Fast-forwarding through most of it, Kelley got to the part where the interviewer asked me—and I had remembered thinking it was a strange question at the time—something about the Civil Rights Act. My reply was, "I like the Civil Rights Act in the sense that it ended discrimination in all public domains, and I'm all in favor of that." In response, the interviewer then asked me about private domains. I laughed and then proceeded to do what most candidates wouldn't— have a philosophical discussion about the federal government mandating rules on private businesses.

I talked about the obvious fact that the federal government has often gone too far in regulating the lives of most citizens and businesses, with much of my discussion with the *Courier-Journal* staff centered on First Amendment issues, an obvious concern for reporters. But honestly, what about the private property rights of most individuals and business owners? Has government gone too far? One of the most egregious examples I like to bring up was a lawsuit brought against a Chipotle Mexican Grill, where a man in wheelchair came in and complained that he could not see his burrito being made. The employees offered to accommodate the man by making his burrito for him at his table. He refused and sued the restaurant chain under the Americans with Disabilities Act. Every one of their nationwide franchises could potentially be forced to lower counter levels. It would later come out that this man was part of a group of professional shakedown artists who specialized in manipulating the legal system for their own gain.

Reasonable people would likely agree that this is a bit extreme, and that questioning the wisdom of such decisions doesn't equal wanting to reinstitute segregation or, as I would also wrongly be charged with, wanting to repeal the ADA.

Reasonable people would also likely agree that when it comes to the government deciding what qualifies as eminent domain, one recent court ruling had stretched that definition to a dangerous extreme. Many Americans were disturbed by the *Kelo v. New London* decision in 2005 in which the Supreme Court had determined that the concept of eminent domain could be broadened to mean anything government might consider a better revenue source. In other words, eminent domain didn't simply mean being forced to sell your property to make way for a bridge or road anymore but it could include an office building, a golf course, a shopping mall—or any other commercial venture that might put more tax dollars in the city's coffers. Think about it, the forced sale of one individual's private property to another private individual—arranged and enforced by the local government. This decision was unprecedented in our nation's history and would have disturbed the Founding Fathers to their very core. Outraged, everyone from the AARP to the NAACP came out against this decision, the latter of which could hardly be accused of wanting to bring back Jim Crow due to their concern over private property rights.

Nevertheless, the *Courier-Journal* reporter would bring our conversation about private property rights back to the realities of life in 1964, and said, "But it's different with race, because much of the discrimination based on race was codified into law." I agreed with him and ended the discussion by saying, "Exactly, it was institutionalized. And that's why we had to end all institutional racism, and I'm completely in favor of that." This interview was available in its entirety on the *Courier-Journal* website. Never did I say I was in favor of repealing the Civil Rights Act. Not once. Yet, this would not stop Conway from repeating the lie as fact on *Hardball* and Ed Schultz's show for several hours. Matthews, to his credit, corrected the record on his show the next day and explained to his audience that I had never called for the repeal of the Civil Rights Act.

When I walked in the house, I was perturbed and told Kelley I would go on the air to clear things up. She told me, "Cancel Rachel Maddow, it's a set-up." But I was feeling my oats. I had a 24-point victory and even America's most left-wing announcer couldn't stop me. I was invincible.

Maddow began the program with an introduction documentary that painted the picture she wanted, intended as an introduction to her eventual line of questioning about my position on the Civil Rights Act of 1964. (I couldn't see or hear any of this due to the satellite feed and wouldn't be made aware of it until later.) It didn't seem to matter that I had never once broached the subject in hundreds of speeches. It was not a subject that anyone, anywhere had been discussing to change legislatively or otherwise. It was, plain and simple, a way to trash me, trash the Tea Party, and to try to derail the momentum of our victory.

We were asked to be on Maddow's program for a short, five-to-seven minute interview about last night's victory. Instead we were sandbagged—the interview was over twenty minutes and not at all about our victory. I reiterated my previous statements that I abhorred racism or discrimination of any kind, that I admired Martin Luther King Jr., particularly his belief that we should be judged not by the color of our skin but the content of our character. I told her what I liked about the Civil Rights Act, that it ended institutional racism in all government schools and transportation.

But Maddow had an agenda. She wanted to talk about

private lunch counters. Did I support segregated lunch counters? I said "no," and that I would never frequent any restaurant or private club that discriminated. But no matter, this line of questioning would go on and on. Obama's one-time preacher Jeremiah Wright, who had said some legitimately and probably intentionally controversial things, had never been put through an interview like this. Perhaps the liberal reporters and bloggers who had been a part of Journolist made sure this never happened, as they once said they might, in much the same way some of them believed calling conservatives "racist" without any basis was a legitimate journalistic tactic. It should be noted that Journolist's Spencer Ackerman was a frequent guest on *The Rachel Maddow Show.*

I don't think most people understood that the controversy was a concerted effort by the other side to drag me into an irrelevant discussion about long-settled legislation simply to peg me as a racist. This controversy didn't happen by accident, but by design. This wasn't about me making a gaffe, but the other side scoring points. In retrospect, the biggest mistake I made was thinking I could go on a liberal network and be treated fairly. At *The American Conservative*, author Thomas E. Woods Jr. wrote a biting response to my critics:

> The Left is going after Rand Paul over the 1964 Civil Rights Act....Rand Paul secretly wants to repeal it, they say, which means we'd have segregated restaurants all over again. Now any non-hysteric knows a segregated restaurant would be boycotted and picketed out of existence within ten seconds, but we're supposed to fret about fictional outcomes from the repeal of a law that will never be repealed.

Woods' comments demonstrated the ridiculousness of the charges and the whole absurdity of the controversy, but this is simply what the Left does to conservatives and, especially, the Tea Party.

The media would pile on for a few days, and the whole episode reminded me of when my primary opponent was trying to claim I was pro-choice. In the end, I guess any lie will do when one's opponents are desperate to destroy you. On the day after the Maddow interview, the pile-on became worse, and every news outlet was not talking about my underdog primary victory but this absurd non-issue. Pundits and anchors were salivating over my "gaffe" with seeming malice.

When I came home that afternoon, my wife told me I looked terrible. I had droopy pouches under my eyes and my skin was pale. I tried to remain upbeat. I'd gone on CNN with Wolf Blitzer and felt that I had explained my position well. But I could tell my wife was starting to get annoyed. She thought I wasn't expressing myself well. Kelley said I just needed to stop with the interviews for a while, and while I didn't necessarily disagree, I was up the next morning at 4 AM and went on *Good Morning America*. Kelley said it was one of my worst interviews yet. She said I usually spoke much better, but in the last few days each interview seemed like a stream-of-consciousness riffing on themes, not a solid counter to the endless accusations about the controversy. She said I was trying to be reasonable when my critics were more interested in a 24/7 news cycle. At one point, Kelley became so annoyed with my stubbornness that she got up from the couch and walked away.

The next morning my wife called me at work and asked me to come home for lunch. She told me again that I needed to take a break from the national interviews. She said I wasn't doing myself any favors. I told Kelley I was scheduled to go on *Meet the Press* on Sunday. "No way," she said. "You know that Duncan is being confirmed on Sunday." With all the craziness, I had forgotten my son's confirmation. Kelley wasn't upset about it, as we'd been thinking of nothing else but the election for the previous two weeks and she had been holding down the fort as far as family matters were concerned. I told her, "You're right, I'll cancel. I'm not missing Duncan's confirmation." I then added, "But you know they're going to crucify me." Kelley said, "Who cares? They already have, and anyway you'll be safest in church."

That evening we all attended Duncan's eighth-grade graduation from St. Joseph School. Duncan, like his brothers, had attended St. Joseph since he was a preschooler. As we sat in the beautiful gothic cathedral, I could see that Kelley was crying. It was an emotional event and both my wife and I were extremely proud of our son. Sitting in church with my family was certainly the best part of that week and eventually, what had been the biggest controversy of the campaign would soon be behind us.

Besides the absurd charge that I was some sort of secret racist, another thing that bothered me about the controversy is it was a reminder of just how limited we are in our public discourse. As my dad often had to deal with in his 2008 presidential campaign, any outside-the-box or unconventional thinking is either dismissed or used to malign one's character. Yet, it's hard to imagine changing the status quo by only considering solutions acceptable to the status quo, and there will need to be something better than the same old political discussions to fix the same old politics.

The Need for Philosopher-Statesmen

When an article about me in *Details* magazine came out, Kelley picked up a couple of copies at the grocery store. After picking up our youngest son, Robert, from tennis practice, she handed him the article, which featured a photo of Robert, Kelley and me eating lunch on the day of the primary. Robert got a huge grin on his face when he saw the picture, with him seated prominently in the foreground taking a big bite out of a Buffalo chicken wing. Typical of Robert, he retreated quietly and immediately started devouring the article.

A minute later, he piped up from the backseat, "Mom, what's an 'infamous wing nut'?"

Kelley responded, "Well, it's somebody who's famous for being a lunatic, I guess."

"Why are they calling me a lunatic?" Robert asked indignantly.

"Honey, they're calling your dad the 'infamous wingnut,' not you!"

"Are you sure?" he asked.

"Of course!" she replied.

Robert finished, "I don't know, I'm the one eating wings!"

The idea that I was a "wing nut" or "crazy" or somehow "not ready for prime time" due to my politics was a narrative that would be spun throughout the election, by both the Left and the Republican establishment. But this notion that my constitutional, limited government message was somehow impractical or unsuitable for today's politics missed the larger point—constitutional, limited government principles must be applied to the mess we now find ourselves in precisely because the status quo is impractical. Economic reality has dictated that the current size of our government is unsustainable. It doesn't make you "out of your mind" to recognize that we are out of money. Democrats who still want to grow government and Republicans who want to help them are essentially useless, no matter how adept they are at making the trains run on time in Washington.

During the election, the media would pick apart the various Tea Party candidates, including me, portraying us as oddballs, weirdos, or outsiders. I can't necessarily defend, nor do I necessarily agree with, what others in the movement have always done or said. But when there's a real movement made up of real people—ordinary, average Americans, not professional pundits or politicians—sometimes "real" people might say or do things that might not pass muster at *The New York Times*. Not surprisingly, most of the Tea Party's politics also don't pass muster at the *Times*, and that's the point—the movement is a challenge and a counter to the so-called "mainstream." It's absurd to always criticize Tea Partiers for thinking outside the box when the movement exists precisely to break down that box. To deplore big government is not "crazy." To champion property rights does not make one a "wing nut," infamous or otherwise.

The American Conservative's Jack Hunter put supposed "wing nuts" like me or my dad into a larger political context, and demonstrates the need for what he calls "philosopher-statesman":

The notion of the philosopher-statesman might be alien to the pundits and hacks who dominate today's politics, but wasn't unusual to the Founding Fathers, many of whom saw themselves in the same light. In our history, when the philosophy of Karl Marx has been implemented through legislation the Left always calls it "progress," but if Ron or Rand Paul dare revisit the philosophy of Thomas Jefferson, we are told they are not ready for "prime time" and should retreat to the libertarian ghetto from which they came. But the exact opposite is true— we all know that the supposed grownups in charge know how to win elections and make modern politics function, but to what end, what good and what function? It is hard to imagine challenging a status quo that almost everyone agrees needs challenging, without first questioning the statist consensus on which it has been built.

When the *Enquirer*, the largest newspaper in northern Kentucky, endorsed my campaign, their statement made many of the same points concerning the dire need for politicians to finally see the big picture—and how doing so often brings controversy for such politicians:

The world would be a poorer place if we did not make room for people with the courage to question conventional wisdom and the smarts to make a cogent case for their own vision. The race for Kentucky's U.S. Senate seat this fall has such a candidate—Republican standard-bearer Rand Paul. Unlike Conway, Paul doesn't fit the mold of a typical politician, and his provocative candor in advancing conservative viewpoints sometimes gets him in trouble...Few candidates we've talked to in recent years have displayed such refreshing intelligence, inquisitiveness and candor. And few candidates have had their words and ideas so frequently vilified and taken out of

context. The real point: Paul is saying things that need
to be said. He is raising issues that at least ought to be
addressed thoughtfully. He is asking questions that
don't-rock-the-boat politicians dare not ask....We need
that kind of voice in the Senate, where too many members indulge in the kind of go-along, get-along group-
think that has allowed government to grow fatter, more
inefficient and more intrusive.

The *Enquirer* added in its endorsement, "A self-proclaimed
'constitutional conservative,' Paul will sometimes defy—and
frustrate—party labels....He won't be pigeonholed."

As evidenced by not only the liberal reaction to my conversations about property rights, but the Republican establishment's milquetoast notion of what passes for "conservative"
these days, we must finally question party labels, what they
mean, and what they should mean, no matter how much it
frustrates party leaders. As evidenced by the Bush years, conservatives have been adrift for too long. The old politics and
politicians must be defied and discarded. And if constitutional
conservatives are going to take America back, they must first
re-examine and reclaim American conservatism.

6

★ ★ ★

Constitutional Conservatism

Barack Obama's campaign promise of change did not include a pledge to transform American conservatism.... The rise of the Tea Party movement is a throwback to an old form of libertarianism that sees most of the domestic policies that government has undertaken since the New Deal as unconstitutional.... The language of the new anti-statists, like the language of the 1950s' right, regularly harks back to the U.S. Constitution and the Founders in calling attention to perceived threats to liberty.... Obama brought back to life a venerable if disturbing style of conservative thinking. In the short run, the new movement's energy threatens him. In the long run, its extremism may be his salvation.

E. J. Dionne Jr., "The Right's New Disturbing Anti-Statists," RealClearPolitics.com, June 21, 2010

* * *

The rise of the Tea Party has been seen as "disturbing" to many critics precisely because its message threatens Obama's agenda. Not surprisingly, these critics rarely consider the rapid growth of government disturbing, too "extreme" or "radical," but any serious efforts to reduce government are always portrayed as "dangerous," undesirable or simply beyond the pale. These critics also see the Tea Party as being primarily a reaction to Obama, and this is half true—this president's ongoing debt avalanche makes his big government agenda the most ambitious and damaging to date. But the Tea Party does not seek to simply go back to the Bush years when the debt was a mere $12 trillion as opposed to $13 trillion. Nor does the Tea Party seek simply to return to the same old Republican rhetoric where limited government was promised but never delivered, the Constitution was referenced but never followed and the Founding Fathers were quoted but never heeded. Mr. Dionne and similar critics are correct to note that the Tea Party movement represents a conservatism rooted in the Founding that is suspect of big government in all its forms. They are also right when they note that the Tea Party is not some unusual deviation in the history of American conservatism, but a return to it.

Extremism in the Defense of Liberty

> *I would remind you that extremism in the defense of liberty is no vice. And let me remind you also that moderation in the pursuit of justice is no virtue.*
>
> Barry Goldwater

Today it has become fashionable to refer to the Republicans as the "party of no." Liberal *New York Times* columnist Frank Rich says the Tea Party takes this position a step further, and perhaps, too far:

> Most Tea Party groups have no affiliation with the G.O.P. despite the party's ham-handed efforts to co-opt them. The more we learn about the Tea Partiers, the more we can see why. They loathe John McCain and the free-spending, TARP-tainted presidency of George W. Bush. They really do hate all of Washington, and if they hate Obama more than the Republican establishment, it's only by a hair or two. The Tea Partiers want to eliminate most government agencies, starting with the Fed and the I.R.S., and end spending on entitlement programs. They are not to be confused with the Party of No holding forth in Washington—a party that, after all, is now positioning itself as a defender of Medicare spending. What we are talking about here is the Party of No Government at All.

To be accurate, the Tea Party stands for limiting government, not "no" government and certainly not "no government at all." The entire purpose of the Constitution was to limit the power the federal government had over the states and the people, where a bicameral legislature would keep checks and balances against itself as well as the executive branch. The Bill of Rights, too, would be another bulwark against overreaching federal power, providing a list of rights reserved to the states and the people, with the Ninth and Tenth amendments underscoring this fact. The Tenth Amendment says explicitly that "The powers not delegated to the United States by the Constitution, nor prohibited by it to the States, are reserved to the States respectively, or to the people."

So strong is the regard for the Tenth Amendment, that various offshoots of the Tea Party have formed completely devoted to it. We held one Tea Party in the state capital with several hundred people chanting, "Where is Jack? Where is Jack?" calling on my opponent, Kentucky's attorney general, to come to the rotunda and explain why he would not join the lawsuit to question the constitutionality of Obamacare.

The legitimate functions of the federal government were outlined in Article 1, Section 8 of the Constitution, some expanded by subsequent amendments, but the extent to which Washington, DC, has ventured outside its constitutional box—this is what the Tea Party now stands against. Does this include questioning the power given to institutions like the Federal Reserve or the Internal Revenue Service, as Rich suggests? Yes it does. Does being a constitutional conservative mean questioning where the federal government gets its authority to intervene in the economy, manage education or mandate healthcare? Certainly. When House Speaker Nancy Pelosi was asked by a reporter in 2009 what part of the Constitution authorized Congress to force Americans to buy health insurance, she replied condescendingly, "Are you serious?" Once again, the Tea Party's answer is a resounding "yes!"

When compared to the entrenched statism of today's status quo, following the Constitution is indeed "extreme" and heeding the Founders is no doubt radical, but it's also the very heart of traditional American conservatism. At one of my early speeches in New York City at Webster Hall, I recited these lines from Goldwater's *Conscience of a Conservative*, a passage that I feel represents the origins of the modern conservative movement:

> The turn will come when we entrust the conduct of our affairs to the men who understand that their first duty as public officials is to divest themselves of the power that they have been given. It will come when Americans, in hundreds of communities throughout the nation, decide to put the man in office who is pledged to enforce the Constitution and restore the Republic. Who will proclaim in a campaign speech: "I have little interest in streamlining government or in making it more efficient, for I mean to reduce its size. I do not undertake to promote welfare, for I propose to extend freedom. My aim is not to pass laws, but to repeal them. It is not to inaugurate new programs, but to cancel the old ones that do violence to the Constitution, or that have failed in their purpose, or that impose on the people an unwarranted financial burden. I will not attempt to discover whether legislation is 'needed' before I have first determined whether it is constitutionally permissible. And if I should later be attacked for neglecting my constituents'

"interests," I shall reply that I was informed their main interest is liberty and that in that cause I am doing the very best I can.

Goldwater's words are a near perfect explanation of constitutional conservatism and the Tea Party might have this passage as its charter, if the movement were actually structured enough to have a charter. Goldwater would have admired the Tea Party's decentralized nature, as the Jeffersonian senator also saw America's hope, not in Washington, DC, but in the "hundreds of communities throughout the nation" which might take back their country by restoring the Old Republic.

In addition to being called a Tea Partier or a constitutional conservative, I've also been called a "Goldwater conservative" by supporters and critics. It is both accurate and an honor to be described as such, not only because Goldwater's philosophy so closely mirrors my own, but when *Conscience of a Conservative* came out in 1960 it was published in the small town of Shepherdsville, Kentucky.

I have also often been called a libertarian. This label is accurate to the degree that I have always been a champion of liberty. It is not accurate to the degree that some of my critics seem to think that the term is pejorative or something alien or even antithetical to conservatism. I have always found this criticism bizarre. It's hard to fathom being a conservative without also, in some manner or respect, being a libertarian. It is also hard to imagine libertarianism being absent or extracted from the American conservative tradition.

Conservatism, Libertarianism, Constitutionalism

I believe the very heart and soul of conservatism is libertarianism.

Ronald Reagan

After winning the primary, I wrote a column for *USA Today* entitled "Rand Paul, libertarian? not quite" in which I explained where libertarianism fits into my philosophy:

It's often repeated in stories about me or my race for U.S. Senate that I am a "libertarian." In my mind, the word "libertarian" has become an emotionally charged, and often misunderstood, word in our current political climate. But, I would argue very strongly that the vast coalition of Americans—including independents, moderates, Republicans, conservatives and "Tea Party" activists—share many libertarian points of view, as do I...I choose to use a different phrase to describe my beliefs— I consider myself a constitutional conservative, which I take to mean a conservative who actually believes in smaller government and more individual freedom. The libertarian principles of limited government, self-reliance and respect for the Constitution are embedded within my constitutional conservatism, and in the views of countless Americans from across the political spectrum. Our Founding Fathers were clearly libertarians, and constructed a Republic with strict limits on government power designed to protect the rights and freedom of the citizens above all else.

This basic, nuts-and-bolts understanding of the individualist philosophy of the Founders could be described as either libertarian or conservative and both would be accurate. In 1976, Ronald Reagan would argue along the same lines: "The basis of conservatism is a desire for less government interference or less centralized authority or more individual freedom and this is a pretty general description also of what libertarianism is... I think that libertarianism and conservatism are traveling the same path."

This path was something Reagan knew well, and many consider his 1964 speech in support of Goldwater's presidential campaign the beginning of Reagan's political career. Often referred to as "Mr. Conservative," Goldwater was also considered a hero to libertarians. FOX News' Judge Andrew Napolitano even dedicated his last book to Goldwater, calling him the father of the American libertarian movement.

Author George H. Nash's *The Conservative Intellectual Movement in America* is widely considered to be the most comprehensive history of American conservatism, and his book starts with libertarianism. Beginning his history, Nash wrote, "For those who believed in the creed of old-fashioned, classical, 19th-century liberal individualism, 1945 was especially lonely, unpromising, and bleak. Free markets, private property, limited government, self reliance, laissez-faire—it had been a long time since principles like these guided government and persuaded peoples." Nash would then focus on the men who would rise to champion these principles, like libertarian economists F. A. Hayek and Ludwig von Mises, or even the more radically libertarian intellectual Albert Jay Nock. Noting the impression Nock made on a young William F. Buckley, Nash wrote, "it was Nockian libertarianism, in fact, which exercised the first conservative influence on the future editor of *National Review*." As for Mises and Hayek, today some of the greatest free market thinkers belong to the Ludwig von Mises Institute in Auburn, Alabama, and talk show host Glenn Beck recently praised Hayek's book *The Road to Serfdom*, saying, "Hayek explained that capitalism is the only system of economics compatible with human dignity, prosperity, and liberty. He demonstrated that planned economies that tried to control the nature of man through administrative rules was impossible, and could only lead to one outcome: Serfdom."

Beck is one of the most popular conservative talk show hosts in the country. He is also a self-described libertarian.

And though I am a self-described constitutional conservative, saying that libertarianism isn't conservatism is like saying communism isn't socialism or progressivism isn't liberalism—yet, it's amusing the degree to which some people still seem to think that the two philosophies are incompatible or exclusive. Fending off some testy Tea Partiers at a town hall last year, Sen. Lindsey Graham told the audience, "I am not a libertarian. If you are, you're welcome to vote for me and build this party, but we're not going to build this party around libertarian ideas." Can we not build the Republican Party around the ideas of Goldwater or Reagan, Hayek or Mises, Buckley or Beck, due to each of these men's libertarian proclivities? If Graham's Republican Party has no room for libertarian ideas, the senator doesn't hold out much hope for the Tea Party either, telling *The New York Times*, "The problem with the Tea Party, I think it's just unsustainable because they can never come up with a coherent vision for governing the country. It will die out." Graham would also tell Tea Partiers: "We're not going to be the Ron Paul party.... I love this party.... I'm not going to let it be hijacked by Ron Paul."

Perish the thought. My dad has been arguably the most constitutionally conservative Republican on Capitol Hill for decades, his ideas are now finding unprecedented popularity in the Tea Party and, to some degree, Dad's philosophy is already "hijacking" the GOP, much like Goldwater and Reagan did decades earlier. The Tea Party keeps growing. If anything, it is the old Republican guard's philosophy that is dying out.

Without the Tea Party, the Republican Party might have completely lost its soul, just like, as Reagan once pointed out— without libertarianism, the conservative movement would lose its heart.

Just Follow the Constitution

In questions of power, then, let no more be heard of confidence in man, but bind him down from mischief by the chains of the Constitution.
Thomas Jefferson

In his introductory remarks during the first Republican debate of the 2008 presidential campaign, my dad said: "Hello, my name is Ron Paul. I am a Congressman from Texas serving in my tenth term. I am the champion of the Constitution." As I've explained, the entire purpose of our Constitution is to limit the federal government in a way in which overly "confident" men would never be allowed to assume too much power because the "chains of the Constitution" would bind them down. My dad's nickname on Capitol Hill is "Dr. No," due to his constant refusal to vote for so much legislation—if it's not in the Constitution, Dad simply will not vote for it. To him, that's what being a "champion of the Constitution" means. Jefferson would have agreed.

Some find this position extreme, but consider for a moment just how extreme our current federal government is. We already know Nancy Pelosi doesn't think the Constitution has any bearing on whether or not she has the power to mandate that Americans purchase health insurance. When Supreme Court Justice Elena Kagan was asked by Sen. Tom Coburn during her confirmation hearings whether or not the federal government could force every American to eat three vegetables a day, she answered honestly—she said yes. According to both Pelosi and Kagan, our federal government is virtually limitless. This view of unlimited federal power negates the entire purpose of the Constitution. Critics like to attack the Tea Party for lacking a "coherent vision for governing the country," yet Washington leaders continue to govern in violation of the very charter they swore to uphold, even mocking it, per Pelosi's example.

Decades of Washington leaders ignoring the Constitution has given rise to more bureaucracy, debt and government centralization culminating in the federal monstrosity we see today. Or as I explained in *USA Today*:

Our current economic crisis, the recent bailouts and the overreach of the one-party rule in Washington have crystallized something for millions of Americans—that something has gone terribly wrong. And it didn't start in 2008. It goes back decades. More and more power became centralized in Washington, D.C., as the federal government responded to every new crisis—from the Great Depression to the Great Recession of today—by expanding its reach deeper into all of our lives. Now Washington forces us to buy health insurance while limiting our choices. Programs must fit its bureaucratic standards, effectively putting government in control of what medicines and treatments millions of Americans can get. The bailouts and federal takeovers of the past two years have made the federal government the nation's top mortgage lender and a major player in auto manufacturing, as well as Wall Street's ATM of first and last resort. This departure from the limited government envisioned by the Founders has encouraged too many Americans to forget their heritage of freedom. When there is a problem, Washington tells us, more government is the solution.

Reagan's axiom that government wasn't the solution to our problems but the problem itself was never heeded, and government exploded not only during his administration, but under each subsequent president, both Republican and Democrat. The notion that thirteen colonies could be ruled exclusively by one central government was anathema to the Founding Fathers and yet today our leaders insist that a nation of 300 million can—and must—be ruled by Washington, DC. This was never the Founders' intention, or as I wrote in *USA Today*: "What the Founders intended…is something different: a federal system that keeps decision-making close to the people. The federal government should not do what the states can do for themselves, the states should not do what local governments can do for themselves, and local governments should not do what families, faith groups and individuals can do for themselves."

This is not anarchy or the "party of no government at all," as some have suggested—simply a limiting of power and delegation of proper government roles. I continued to explain the Founding Fathers' vision of constitutional balance:

> The Founders understood, however, that the federal government has important roles to play, both in protecting our nation and in protecting the rights of its citizens. State and local governments can exceed their powers and injure citizens' rights just as the federal government can. That's why the Constitution explicitly forbids states to do certain things, such as issue their own currency. Before the Constitution was ratified, states created inflationary currencies to defraud creditors. Sometimes federal action is necessary to correct violations of rights at the state and local levels. Liberty is secure in a federal system when the federal government and the states check one another, not when either side completely dominates the other at the expense of freedom.

This system of balancing federal and state power is integral to understanding the nature and purpose of the Constitution. Jefferson believed that if any proposed legislation was not authorized in Article 1, Section 8 then it was simply unconstitutional. Jefferson also believed that the Tenth Amendment was the key to understanding our entire system of government. For the "Sage of Monticello," the Tenth Amendment was not simply one amendment among many but a restatement of the Constitution's expressed purpose and the federal government's necessary limits, if the republic was to survive.

Not surprisingly, the Tenth Amendment is routinely ignored

while certain aspects of the Constitution, like the Commerce Clause, have been so expanded in their definition that they can mean anything. Former federal judge Andrew Napolitano is an authority on the history of the Supreme Court (his book *The Constitution in Exile* is a great tool in this area), and particularly the last seventy years in which there has been such a gross expansion of the definition and scope of the Commerce Clause. Napolitano explained this expansion during a speech before *Campaign for Liberty* in 2009:

> To "regulate" meant to keep "regular," it meant to make sure that there is commerce between the states. Not to allow the Congress to regulate everything under the sun, like the conditions of employment or the hourly wages, or the materials used to make up an article that moves in interstate commerce, but just to make sure that interstate commerce is "regular." To prevent, for example, the state of Pennsylvania from saying to merchants in New Jersey "you can't sell your goods here, only local merchants in Pennsylvania can sell them." That's what the commerce clause was written for. But Congress, of course, has used it to regulate the air that you breathe, the water that you drink, the force of the shower in your home, the size of your toilet bowl, and the number of legs on your desk chair, and on and on and on.

The modern understanding of the Commerce Clause is so damaged that my opponent in the general election, Kentucky's attorney general, went on national television and argued that Obamacare had to be constitutional because nowhere in the Constitution did it say that you had a right not to have insurance. My response was "What law school did he attend?" To not understand that the Constitution is not a complete listing of your individual rights, to not understand that the Ninth Amendment clearly says that those rights that are not listed are not to be disparaged, is to disqualify a person from office. I told him this, much to the delight of Tea Party audiences across Kentucky.

To demonstrate just how egregious the federal government has become in its abuse of the Commerce Clause, when Rep. James Clyburn was a guest on Napolitano's "Freedom Watch" program on *FOX Business*, he was asked what gave the federal government the authority to regulate or administer healthcare. The Congressman was honest about it: "There's nothing in the Constitution that says that the federal government has anything to do with most of the stuff we do." Even so, Democrats like Pelosi and other liberals cite the Commerce Clause as an excuse for Obamacare, as if the Founders ever intended any such thing.

It's not hard to imagine what Jefferson or any of the Founders would think about the federal government forcing Americans to purchase healthcare or demanding that citizens eat three vegetables a day. It's also not hard to imagine what they would think of the federal government trying to run education, which is not in the Constitution, and the Department of Education should be abolished. The department was created during the Carter administration, was opposed by Reagan and as late as 1996 the Republican platform read, "The Federal government has no constitutional authority to be involved in school curricula or to control jobs in the market place. This is why we will abolish the Department of Education, end federal meddling in our schools, and promote family choice at all levels of learning." Five years later President Bush would double the department by signing into law No Child Left Behind, which established greater federal involvement in education through mandated standardized testing. None of this federal involvement would improve education or as the *Reason Foundation* recently noted in a cumulative analysis of government programs "the president has proposed a $78 billion education budget for 2011, a whopping $18.6 billion more than in 2010. Federal education spending has increased by close to 80 percent in real terms since 2001, but test scores in reading and math among 17-year-olds have been flat since 1971, according to the National Assessment of Education Progress." In his article for the Cato Institute, "All Americans Left Behind," Andrew J. Coulson wrote:

> The Program for International Student Assessment was first administered to 15-year-olds in 2000, testing them on mathematics, reading, and science. Students in the United States earned an overall math score of 493 on the 1,000 point scale, seven points below average, placing us 18th out of the 27 participating countries. Three years later, PISA results showed no significant change in U.S. math performance. But according to the latest report the U.S. suffered a significant decline in mathematics achievement between 2003 and 2006. We now score 474—in 25th place among the 30 participating countries.

In light of such statistics, I know very few teachers who like No Child and don't know any serious conservatives who believe the federal government has any business meddling with our schools. Education should be left to states and local communities, as the Founders intended and the Tenth Amendment demands.

The Department of Energy, also created during the Carter administration, is another example of the federal government becoming too intrusive by overstepping its constitutional bounds. First and foremost, it should be the free market that decides what type of energy we use, not the government. The department was created in 1977 during the oil crisis (notice again, every time there's a crisis government grows) to make sure we had an adequate energy supply, but has evolved beyond this, often actually restricting our energy supply. Like the Department of Education, even when created for supposed safety or reasons of national stability, government departments always grow larger and larger, taking on a life of their own. It's not that I, or any other conservative, is necessarily opposed to some of the functions of these departments, but every time these new bureaucracies are established, their power inevitably and indomitably ends up reaching far beyond what anyone initially intended.

Trading Liberty for Security and Getting Neither

> No government ever voluntarily reduces itself in size. Government programs, once launched, never disappear. Actually, a government bureau is the nearest thing to eternal life we'll ever see on this earth.
> Ronald Reagan

Another example of bloated government inefficiency and over-reach would be the Department of Homeland Security. I, like most Americans, am completely in favor of homeland security. I also would have never voted to establish this government department. Conservative Republicans usually argue that smaller is better when it comes to government, but putting so many preexisting agencies under the banner of the DHS (Transportation Security Administration, The Federal Emergency Management Agency, the Coast Guard, Immigration and Naturalization Services) has certainly not made us any safer or financially sound.

Similar to the creation of other departments, a crisis happens, government steps in, and we are left with a monstrous bureaucracy that is not only unconstitutional but seemingly permanent. On the ninth anniversary of 9/11, CNN's Fareed Zakaria outlined exactly how much new bureaucracy has emerged in the last decade, noting that the federal government has created or reconfigured at least 263 organizations all purportedly related to the war on terror. The dollar amount spent on intelligence is up by 250 percent, amounting to $75 billion—which Zakaria correctly notes is merely a "public number, which is a gross underestimate," adding that this is "more than the rest of the world spends put together." For new bureaucracies related solely to intelligence, there are thirty-three new government buildings occupying 17 million square feet, which would be the equivalent of 22 U.S. Capitol buildings, or three Pentagons. And a $3.4 billion Department of Homeland Security building is being built, making it not only the largest bureaucracy after the Pentagon and Department of Veteran Affairs but, as Zakaria notes, "the largest government site in 50 years," with a workforce of nearly a quarter of a million federal employees.

Like the rest of the Department of Homeland Security, the TSA is also now out of control. One of the legislators who authorized the agency's creation, Rep. John Mica, told FOX News, "The TSA is a federal agency, the last four years, that's been driving off a cliff just like the Congress. . . . We saw that it was growing in size, and some of their overreach . . . it's grown to 67,000 employees, 3,590 administrators just here in Washington, DC, another 8,000 out there, this thing is blown totally out of proportion." Mica now regrets ever signing into legislation the creation of the TSA precisely because it has become just another example of government incompetence, inefficiency, and—as is always the case with government— overreaching intrusiveness.

At the end of 2010, DHS Secretary Janet Napolitano instructed TSA workers to begin patting down airline passengers in a manner some described as "groping" or even "molestation." TSA officials were touching private citizens in intimate areas in ways that would be considered a crime if those doing the groping didn't work for the government. It's not hard to imagine what the Founders would think of this behavior either.

It's also not hard to imagine what the Founders would think of the gloriously misnamed PATRIOT Act, another unconstitutional government intrusion hastily passed by Congress and signed into law by the president in the midst of a crisis. Sometimes conservatives seem to believe that giving the federal government unprecedented power in spying or warrantless wiretapping is somehow a positive development, but this is exactly the sort of intrusiveness the Founders feared most, particularly given their experience with the British. This sort of invasiveness is also precisely the reason we have a Second Amendment protecting our right to keep and bear arms, or as Jefferson wrote "The strongest reason for the people to retain the right to keep and bear arms is, as a last resort, to protect themselves against tyranny in government."

Conservatives have no problem defending the Second Amendment but often seem to forget about defending the Fourth Amendment which reads, "The right of the people to be secure in their persons, houses, papers, and effects, against unreasonable searches and seizures, shall not be violated, and no Warrants shall issue, but upon probable cause, supported by Oath or affirmation, and particularly describing the place to be searched, and the persons or things to be seized."

During the campaign, I had the opportunity to speak at the Knob Creek Machine Gun Shootout, the largest collection of gun owners and machine gun enthusiasts ever assembled. Over five thousand people gather each day of the event to shoot old jalopies on cinder blocks or target explosive canisters. People travel from all over the United States to attend this event. In my speech, I reminded conservatives that we cannot adequately protect the Second Amendment if we don't protect other, equally important amendments. For example, attempts to limit the First Amendment or free speech, like McCain–Feingold (so-called "campaign finance reform"), infringe on our ability to speak out and defend gun rights. Likewise, attempts to lessen the requirements for a search warrant infringe on the Fourth Amendment, making it more possible for gun rights to be trampled upon. I told the gun enthusiasts that unless you want a government that can enter your house at will, check to see if you have trigger locks, measure the length of your guns and rapidity of their ability to fire, you must oppose violations of the Fourth Amendment like the PATRIOT Act. My primary opponent tried to use my opposition to the PATRIOT Act against me, but once I responded by demonstrating that the Second Amendment could not be protected without the First and Fourth, no conservative questioned my position.

In 2009, the DHS issued a warning that Tea Partiers were an example of "right-wing extremism" and also noted that "heightened interest in legislation for tighter firearms...may be invigorating rightwing extremist activity." Who's to say the Tea Party won't become the government's next target under the PATRIOT Act? Benjamin Franklin once wrote, "They who can give up essential liberty to obtain a little temporary safety, deserve neither liberty nor safety," and Americans who continue to support unconstitutional intrusions into the private lives of their fellow citizens will inevitably learn the same lesson.

It's also worth noting the degree to which these measures are not only infringements on our constitutional liberties, but have been both inefficient and massive engines of government growth. Fareed Zakaria notes in *Newsweek* that "some 30,000 people are now employed exclusively to listen in on phone conversations and other communications in the United States," but even so Army intelligence still did not notice that Maj. Nidal Malik Hasan had been behaving strangely and making threats during his training at Walter Reed Army Medical Center despite repeated warnings about his behavior from Hasan's Nigerian father. Nor did intelligence heed the warnings issued by the Nigerian father of the "underwear" bomber last Christmas, who was unsuccessful due mostly to his own incompetence. Zakaria asks: "The rise of this national-security state has entailed a vast expansion in the government's powers that now touches every aspect of American life, even when seemingly unrelated to terrorism. In the past, the U.S. government has built up for wars, assumed emergency authority, and sometimes abused that power, yet always demobilized after the war. But this is a war without end. When do we declare victory? When do the emergency powers cease?"

Like every aspect of federal expansion, the rise of our national security state represents government growth without end. We should also ask, despite all their groping and intrusive tactics, has the TSA ever caught a single terrorist or intercepted a single bomber? With our vast security apparatus why were there no red flags over Fort Hood terrorist Nidal Malik Hasan or intelligence sharing concerning the Christmas Day underwear bomber? Why, a decade after 9/11, has government not come up with a better method of recognizing frequent flyers and cutting down on unnecessary inconvenience, something a privatized system would have likely already accomplished? Why has the federal government not better addressed our porous borders and illegal immigration problem with the same level of focus it now devotes to policing American citizens who choose to travel? For what reason are our grandparents being harassed every time they go on vacation, how much are we spending to be treated in this manner, and when, exactly, will our lives return to normal?

Returning to the Constitution will necessarily mean seriously reducing, substantively reforming or even abolishing much of the national security state, the national education state, the national energy state, the national healthcare state, and countless other areas in which our federal government has drastically overstepped its constitutional boundaries. The level of mandates and regulation Americans tolerate today would have never been tolerated by the Founders and the Constitution's explicit purpose was to prevent such a turn of events from ever unfolding. We must return to the virtues this nation was founded upon: hard work, individual responsibility, families and neighbors taking care of one another, and honest competition in the marketplace—most of which are always hampered and rarely helped by government involvement.

It was virtues such as these that helped build this nation, and we must not allow our government to destroy us from within. Neither can we allow our government to destroy us from without by constantly devoting our blood, treasure and resources to the building of other nations.

7

★ ★ ★

A Conservative Foreign Policy

Counterinsurgency, as defined by McChrystal's successor, Gen. David Petraeus and tepidly embraced by Barack Obama for a year or so, does not just involve nation-building, it is nation-building. This does not just require political acumen, it requires the wisdom of Aristotle, the leadership skills of George Washington and the analytic sophistication of Tocqueville. But, then, the grinding paradox of nation-building is this: No one with the aptitudes necessary for it would be rash or delusional enough to try it.

—George F. Will, columnist

* * *

Many Republicans treat war like Democrats treat welfare. No matter how long we fight the War on Poverty—how many billions we spend, what kind of results we get or how many unintended consequences arise—Democrats always insist we must do more. For Republicans to even question government policy on this matter is the quickest way to get accused of not caring about the poor or worse. And so, from generation to generation, dollar to dollar, deficit to deficit, the welfare status quo carries on—unchallenged and undisturbed.

Similarly, no matter how long we fight the War on Terror— how many billions we spend, what kind of results we get or how many unintended consequences arise—Republicans have typically insisted we must do more. To even question government policy on this matter is the quickest way to get accused of being weak on terrorism or worse. And from generation to generation, dollar to dollar, deficit to deficit, the foreign policy status quo carries on—unchallenged and undisturbed.

The great irony is that conservatives preach individual responsibility and reliance domestically but practice policies abroad that create dependence on foreign aid and dependence on foreign soldiers. Where conservatives will ask the domestically unemployed to seek work and become independent of government welfare, abroad we let nations depend on our suc-cor. We don't demand the same self-reliance internationally that we do domestically.

Nobody questions that problems such as poverty or terror-ism are going to be with us for the long haul. But how might we better deter, diminish or spend less on either? Nobody—or very few—seem to be willing to ask these questions, or as I told ABC's *This Week*'s Christiane Amanpour just five days after I became senator-elect: "Republicans traditionally say, 'Oh, we'll cut domestic spending, but we won't touch the military.' The liberals—the ones who are good—will say, 'Oh, we'll cut the military, but we won't cut domestic spending....' Bot-tom line is, you have to look at everything across the board." I added, "National defense is the most important thing we do in Washington, but there's still waste in the military budget. You have to make it smaller. But you also then need to address: how many wars are we going to be involved in? Are we going to be involved in every war all the time?"

Though an integral part of the conservative creed is to ques-tion government, it makes many Republicans nervous to even hint at questioning our foreign policy, particularly when those questions are coming from fellow Republicans. After my com-ments on ABC's *This Week*, Sen. John McCain expressed this long-held establishment view, seeming genuinely worried that I might be coming to Washington to challenge it: "I think there are going to be some tensions within our party. I don't know upcoming senator Rand Paul. I respect and admire his victory, but already he has talked about withdrawals from, or cuts in, defense....There's no doubt that this new group of Republicans have come in with a commitment that we take a meat ax to spending.... So I worry a lot about the rise of protectionism and isolationism in the Republican Party."

Calling me an "isolationist" is about as accurate or appropriate as calling Senator McCain an "imperialist," a characterization I'm sure he would dismiss as readily as I dismiss his. Sen. Tom Coburn, who has also suggested we need to look at defense cuts to reduce the deficit, immediately rejected McCain's charge, responding, "It's not hard to cut the defense budget and keep our defense exactly where it is. That's how much waste is over there. Nothing is sacrosanct; it can't be. As a matter of fact, the way the Defense Department is run now, we're actually getting less bang for the buck. If we trim it down, we'll get more bang for the buck."

As part of the incoming "new group of Republicans," "with a commitment" to "take a meat ax to spending," Congressman Justin Amash has said, "If you want to be serious about cutting the federal budget, we have to look at the Pentagon budget." Also part of the Tea Party "tidal wave" that swept through the midterm elections is Congressman Allen West, who raised some reasonable questions about our foreign policy during an interview with ABC News: "I think we need to look at how we can be successful in these combat theaters of operation. The twenty-first-century battlefield is a totally different battlefield. We have to get away from occupation and nation-building-style warfare...." ABC News asked, "But isn't nation building and occupation building exactly what we're doing with the surge in Afghanistan?" "Absolutely," said West, "That was something that I saw when I was a commander in Iraq and when I was also a civilian military adviser in Afghanistan." ABC News then asked, "Should we be cutting from the defense budget?"

West replied, "I think you have to."

And we do. National security is—bar none—the most important constitutional function of our federal government. It is also not only 40 percent of our budget, but it is a budget larger than every other nation on earth combined spends on defense. In fact, the United States alone represents nearly half the world's defense budget. In the effort to reduce the debt, applying a cost-benefit analysis to every part of the federal government is not only necessary, but long overdue, particularly as it relates to the Pentagon. An increasing number of Republicans are beginning to realize this and calling them or any other conservative who now dares challenge our foreign policy status quo "isolationist" is no different than liberals calling the Tea Party "racist." Both are cuss words designed to end debate and distract from very serious and pressing issues.

The Tea Party senses that the national debt is such a grave threat to our country that we absolutely must become consistent conservatives, conservative with all federal spending, not just domestic spending. According to the chairman of the Joint Chiefs of Staff, Adm. Mike Mullen, "Our national debt is our biggest national security threat." It's time we stopped with the name calling and had an adult conversation about how to best fight this imminent threat.

What Constitutes "National Defense"?

McCain once told me that the United States needs to spend a good deal more than 50 percent of the world's total defense budget....Seeing Rand Paul on CNN a day or two after the election, talking cogently to Wolf Blitzer about how no serious agenda of fiscal responsibility can avoid scaling back military spending, was almost an out-of-body experience. You mean...Republican senators...can say that? Out loud and everything? Well, they used to, and they finally are again....

Matt Welch, editor-in-chief, *Reason* magazine

If, for Democrats, to adjust or address the practicality of a program like Social Security is always tantamount to throwing Grandma out on the street, for too long too many Republicans have used the same fear-mongering approach toward adjusting the defense budget—where merely questioning the foreign policy status quo is portrayed as somehow appeasing our enemies. As I've stated previously, national security is a primary function of our federal government and I even think defense should be the largest part of our budget—a budget many would agree should be reduced overall. Everything must be on the table, and we cannot even begin to control spending without a serious re-assessment of America's military role in the world and how much we're willing to pay for it.

Today, America has troops in over 170 countries and 750 bases around the globe. President Obama has reduced US troop levels in Iraq to 50,000 where, of course, we have been fighting a war. But we also have more American soldiers—well over 60,000—stationed in Germany. Under President Bush, defense spending averaged 3.7 percent of the Gross Domestic Product (GDP). Now, under President Obama, it has reached 4.7 percent of the GDP. The official cost of the wars in Iraq and Afghanistan totals about $1 trillion by some estimates, but economist Joseph Stiglitz has noted that once hidden costs or "non-discretionary spending" is added in—like money borrowed from China or increased veterans' expenses due to these conflicts—about $3 trillion is a more accurate price tag. Of course, we must remember that we are nowhere close to finishing paying for Iraq and, like every other aspect of his spending, President Obama is already on course to outdo Bush in Afghanistan. Tallying up Obama's military budget, the Cato Institute's David Isenberg writes that $708 billion in 2010 "is more than we spent on the Pentagon in any year since 1946—in dollars adjusted for inflation.... Those levels of Pentagon spending do not include what we pay for foreign aid, arms sales and arms control, Veterans, Homeland Security, the Pentagon's share of interest on the national debt, and more. To tally up our entire national security budget, we can get very cozy with $1 trillion."

One of the Tea Party's main rallying cries has been opposition to Obamacare. During the debates over that proposal, Congressman Barney Frank argued that if we hadn't spent a trillion dollars in Iraq we would have enough money for government-run healthcare. Should conservatives' answer be, "No, Congressman Frank, we should be spending $1 trillion or more overseas but never at home," or should it be that we shouldn't be spending trillions, period?

The answer to this question depends on what kind of conservatives we're talking about. I've mentioned before that the big government Republicans who were in control during the Bush administration, or neoconservatives, often measure America's greatness by our ability to maintain a massive global military presence, or what critics have called "policing the world." To suggest that some of these global commitments are perhaps not in our national interest, have nothing to do with actual "defense" or can no longer be afforded—these are conversations neoconservatives and similar-minded Republicans aren't willing to have. McCain's aversion to my questioning our foreign policy status quo reflects this view. So did a *Washington Post* column written by the American Enterprise Institute's (a Washington think tank widely known for hosting many of today's leading neoconservatives) Danielle Pletka and Thomas Donnelly, who argue for increased military spending:

> The road backward beckons in an almost Calvinistic call to fiscal discipline; austerity is its virtue even before national security in a time of war. Libertarians and Tea Party darlings such as Ron and Rand Paul and conservative stalwarts such as Tom Coburn have long inhabited this political territory.... Members of the GOP vanguard such as Indiana Gov. Mitch Daniels and, possibly, insurgent Tea Party candidates are joining them.... Nothing less than a fight for the soul of conservatism is underway. Whereas some, such as Sen. John McCain, despise Pentagon profligacy because they are willing to pay the cost— even in blood—of American international leadership, it appears many young-gun conservatives are from another school, believing those costs are too high.... To them, the Defense Department is another case of wasteful government and bureaucratic collusion that has, in Coburn's words, "allowed the military-industrial complex to make things unaffordable." For others, doctrinaire fiscal conservatism blends easily with a renewed isolationism.

Pletka and Donnelly no doubt embrace the term "neoconservative" as readily as I, my dad, or Senator Coburn embrace "isolationist," but regardless and again, cuss words are no substitute for substantive debate.

Syndicated columnist Pat Buchanan understands well what makes this particular breed of Republican uneasy, writing that the neoconservatives "are nervous the Tea Party may not sign up to soldier on for the empire. Writing in *The Washington Post*, Danielle Pletka and Thomas Donnelly of AEI have sniffed out the unmistakable scent of 'isolationism' among Tea Party favorites." Adds Buchanan, "Sorry, but the old neocon name-calling won't cut it this time."

The Tea Party has already been called every bad name imaginable and will not fall prey to such schoolyard-type goading. We won't be bullied into supporting massive spending needlessly under a Republican brand no matter how badly certain members of the party desire it. As the movement becomes ever more comprehensive in its limited government desires, more questions will inevitably be raised about certain aspects of spending that the old Republican guard once considered untouchable.

The Tea Party must leave nothing untouched.

Ike and the "Military-Industrial Complex"

Secretary Weinberger, I'd like to have a list of bases that you want to close and can close. I don't need it this afternoon but maybe tomorrow morning would be time enough.
Barry Goldwater

The "military-industrial complex" mentioned by Senator Coburn was a term coined by President Dwight Eisenhower during his 1961 farewell address, in which Ike warned: "Until the latest of our world conflicts, the United States had no armaments industry. American makers of plowshares could, with time and as required, make swords as well. But now we can no longer risk emergency improvisation of national defense; we have been compelled to create a permanent armaments industry of vast proportions....We annually spend on military security more than the net income of all United States corporations."

Eisenhower's concern mirrored that of the Founding Fathers, who believed that extending the country militarily, or even the militarization of civilian society, was not conducive to, nor compatible with, republican government. In his farewell address, President George Washington said, "The great rule of conduct for us in regard to foreign nations is, in extending our commercial relations to have with them as little political connection as possible. So far as we have already formed engagements let them be fulfilled with perfect good faith. Here let us stop." James Madison warned that "the greatest danger to liberty is from large standing armies," and Jefferson would take this concern even further, writing that "the spirit of this country is totally adverse to a large military force."

In short, the Founders believed having big government abroad meant having big government at home.

Of course, having to fight two world wars had changed things, but Eisenhower—a five-star general and the supreme commander of the Allied Forces during World War II—worried that "national defense" was quickly becoming more of an excuse, not necessarily a warranted reason, for bigger government. Ike continued in his farewell address: "Our military organization today bears little relation to that known by any of my predecessors in peacetime, or indeed by the fighting men of World War II or Korea. This conjunction of an immense military establishment and a large arms industry is new in the American experience. The total influence—economic, political, even spiritual—is felt in every city, every statehouse, every office of the federal government. We recognize the imperative need for this development. Yet we must not fail to comprehend its grave implications. Our toil, resources, and livelihood are all involved; so is the very structure of our society."

Eisenhower then delivered what became arguably his most famous quote:

In the councils of government, we must guard against the acquisition of unwarranted influence, whether sought or unsought, by the military-industrial complex. The potential for the disastrous rise of misplaced power exists and will persist.

In his last days in office, Eisenhower was heard to remark, "God help any man who sits behind this desk who doesn't know the military like I do."

Ike feared that the "military establishment," like any other government department, might expand or grow beyond what the military was intended for, and that government or corporate interests might begin to dictate policies as opposed to actual defense. How much of the Department of Education today has to do with actually educating our children, and how much of it is an excuse for sustaining a bloated bureaucracy? Likewise, how much of the Department of Defense is dedicated to actual defense? In an article entitled "Was Ike right about the 'military-industrial-complex'?" Harvard professor of international affairs Stephen M. Walt wrote in *Foreign Policy*:

[The Department of Defense] is insulated from serious cuts by an array of impressive political advantages. First, its budget is more than 50 percent of all federal discretionary spending, and its sheer size gives it a lot of bureaucratic clout. Second, the Pentagon has a large domestic constituency: there are 1.4 million men and women in uniform, 850,000 paid members of the National Guard and Reserve, and 650,000 civilian employees. Forget GM, Ford and Chrysler: the Department of Defense is the largest single employer in the whole country. Now add the companies that provide goods and services for the military. Their employees amount to about 5.2 million jobs, which is a pretty impressive domestic constituency.... Finally, a well-financed group of Beltway bandits and Washington think tanks stand ready to question the patriotism of any politician...who tries to put the Pentagon on a diet.

Former CIA counterterrorism specialist Philip Giraldi echoed Walt's points and Eisenhower's concern in a column for *Campaign for Liberty*, explaining his reasons for why the military-industrial complex should be a target for the Tea Party as much as any other part of our government:

Most Tea Partiers claim to want smaller and cheaper government, less interference from Washington in their daily lives, and fewer programs that are intended to socially re-engineer the nation. [But]...it is precisely the interventionist defense and foreign policies that are driving the bad things they see in government....The United States now accounts for 45% of the entire world total for military spending, euphemistically referred to as "defense." The Pentagon budget has gone from $432 billion in 2001 to a projected $720 billion in 2011, not including the costs of the wars in Iraq and Afghanistan. The Federal Government is twice as big as it was in 2001 and there has been the creation of major new bureaucracies at the Department of Homeland Security and the office of the Director of National Intelligence, neither of which can be regarded as a model of efficiency.

Giraldi adds, "There is no good reason for Washington to serve as the world's policeman and many good reasons why it should cease and desist from doing so."

Every American believes in fighting for our national defense. But I suspect few believe we should be policing the world, nation building, or worse—fighting wars abroad in pursuit of utopian ideology.

The Progressive Notion of American Exceptionalism

I think we developed in the Republican Party a—well, you know, the buzzword for it is "neoconism." But I think what it is, it's an ideology—it's really an idealistic approach to things. But it's a combination of idealism and, if you will, brute force.

Brent Scowcroft, former National Security Adviser
to presidents Gerald Ford and George H.W. Bush

After 9/11, America took the battle to our enemies and I would have voted to go to war in Afghanistan because we needed to fight back. There was a clear link between Al-Qaeda and the Taliban and this is exactly what our military is for—national *defense*. Whether we should still be in Afghanistan nation building a decade later is an entirely different matter.

But unlike Afghanistan, I would not have voted to go to war with Iraq, not only because there was no link between Saddam Hussein and 9/11, but because that country did not pose a threat to the United States. The intelligence concerning Iraq supposedly possessing weapons of mass destruction was always questionable at best and the Bush administration's repeated attempts to link Hussein to Al-Qaeda were suspect—and more transparently so when the administration began to deny using such rhetoric. Former Chairman of the Joint Chiefs of Staff Gen. Hugh Shelton was the nation's top military officer when the Iraq War was beginning to take shape behind the scenes, and he expressed his puzzlement about the logic of that war during an interview with ABC's *This Week*'s Christiane Amanpour: "There was a very strong push in those days for us to go into Iraq, and there was absolutely no intelligence, zero, that pointed toward the Iraqis....It was all Al Qaeda, Osama bin Laden. And yet there was an element there that was—that was pushing to go into Iraq at the same time."

The key to understanding why Bush administration officials would push to go to war when it didn't make sense lies in understanding the roots of neoconservative ideology.

During the early and mid-twentieth century, presidents Theodore Roosevelt and Woodrow Wilson would make the case that America should embark on imperial adventures, not unlike the British once did, often combining overseas expansion with an ideology that America should "make the world safe for democracy," to use Wilson's phrase. This was considered a very utopian or liberal worldview. The alternative view was represented by men like Sen. Robert Taft, who was considered the conservative standard-bearer of that era and was called "Mr. Republican" by colleagues. Taft and fellow Republicans believed that America's foreign policy should reflect the national interest and proper defense, not the interests and defense of other nations for ideological purposes. Reflecting George Washington's view that we should not become enmeshed needlessly in "foreign entanglements" or John Quincy Adams' advisement that America should not go "abroad in search of monsters to destroy," Taft made a point to say in 1946 that the wars we participated in—most recently World War II—were fought "to maintain the freedom of our own people.... Certainly, we did not go to war to reform the world."

Interestingly enough, during the 1952 presidential election, Eisenhower, who would later warn of the military-industrial complex, was challenged by Taft in the Republican primaries. Eisenhower was considered the moderate candidate, like Nelson Rockefeller in 1964 or Gerald Ford in 1974, and Taft had the backing of conservative Republicans, much like Goldwater did in 1964 or Reagan in 1976. Today, the fairly conventional foreign policy language of both Eisenhower and Taft, in which both men were always concerned about military cost and overstretch, might sound left-wing if judged by the standards of a Republican Party tainted by neoconservative ideology—just as moderate Republican Eisenhower or conservative Republican Taft would likely have considered today's utopian, neoconservative rhetoric unmistakably liberal.

Today, many neoconservatives take French author Alexis de Tocqueville's notion of "American Exceptionalism" and twist it to mean that the United States must continue to police the world and maintain a permanent global presence, and that our "exceptional" nature justifies this. But America's enduring exceptionalism, or specialness, is something that is enshrined in our documents, from the Declaration of Independence to the Constitution. On election night, I said of American Exceptionalism:

> Why is America great? How did America come to be the richest and freest nation known to history? America is exceptional, not inherently so, but because throughout our history, we embraced freedom. We fought for it. Men and women have died for it. It is the cornerstone of our country: freedom in the economic marketplace and freedom in the political marketplace. America will remain great if we remain proud of the American system, a system that enshrines and protects by law a system of free exchange or capitalism....

But to the degree that we believe it is our mission to remake the world in our image—and that this is somehow American Exceptionalism—is not only a betrayal of the Founders' vision, but a fool's errand. Taft agreed, or as John Moser of the Ashbrook Center writes: "Foremost among the principles that guided Taft's foreign policy was a strong faith in the exceptionalism of America and its people.... Like them, he was convinced that the United States was based on certain noble ideas that placed the nation far above the rest of the world.... Of these ideas, individual liberty was for him the most important; indeed, he proclaimed early and often that the 'principal purpose of the foreign policy of the United States is to maintain the liberty of our people.' He held that there were three fundamental requirements for the maintenance of such liberty—an economic system based on free enterprise, a political system based on democracy, and national independence and sovereignty. All three, he feared, might be destroyed in a war, or even by extensive preparations for war.... The First World War had, he claimed, 'set up more extreme dictatorships than the world had seen for many days.' He was certain that another war would destroy American democracy, creating 'an absolute arbitrary dictatorship in Washington.' "

Taft was correct in the sense that the most massive government growth in our history, at that time at least, would occur during the Wilson and FDR administrations, and the liberal notion that it was America's role to make the world safe for democracy would become a permanent facet of the progressive agenda of that era. Talk show host Glenn Beck has done an outstanding job in educating his audience about the progressive movement and their historical origins, telling his audience in 2009:

I am becoming more and more libertarian every day, I guess the scales are falling off of my eyes, as I'm doing more and more research into history and learning real history. Back at the turn of the century in 1900, with Teddy Roosevelt—a Republican—we started this, "we're going to tell the rest of the world," "we're going to spread democracy," and we really became, down in Latin America, we really became thuggish and brutish. It only got worse with the next progressive that came into office—Teddy Roosevelt, Republican progressive—the next one was a Democratic progressive, Woodrow Wilson, and we did...we empire built. The Democrats felt we needed to empire build with one giant global government....The Republicans took it as, "we're going to lead the world and we'll be the leader of it."...I don't think we should be either of those. I think we need to mind our own business and protect our own people. When somebody hits us, hit back hard, then come home.

When the enemy hit us on 9/11, America wanted to hit back hard, and we did. That's what sending troops to Afghanistan was about in the beginning. But a decade later, we've never come home. We know why we went into Afghanistan—but most Americans are not sure why we're there now.

And we're still not sure why we went to Iraq.

Making the World Safe for Democracy

Americans should not go abroad to slay dragons they do not understand in the name of spreading democracy.
John Quincy Adams

The most magnificently misnamed neoconservatives are the most radical people in this town.
George F. Will, columnist

Though it was supported by most conservatives, the Iraq War was based on liberal premises. In both domestic and foreign policy, this is what the neoconservatives have come to represent—the progressive ideology of presidents Roosevelt or Wilson, repackaged and passed off as "conservative."

The American Conservative's Daniel McCarthy notes the ideology's early socialist roots, writing: "The Trotskyist pedigree of neoconservatism is no secret; the original neocon, Irving Kristol, acknowledges it with relish: 'I regard myself to have been a young Trostkyite and I have not a single bitter memory.'" (The late Kristol further popularized the term *neoconservative* by fully embracing it, and was the father of *Weekly Standard* editor William Kristol). McCarthy adds:

> It's also worth noting that the neoconservative preoccupation with exporting social democracy abroad through war and mercantilism reflects the original split between Trotsky and Stalin. Trotsky argued that there could not be "socialism in one country" but rather that the revolution had to be truly international. And so the neoconservatives push for "human rights" and social democratic governments to be imposed…by force of arms….We're still fighting to make the world safe for (social) democracy. Somewhere in the bowels of hell Leon Trotsky must be smiling.

Author Michael Kazin demonstrated well how the rhetoric used to sell the Iraq War reflected this socialist or progressive, universalist vision. In a 2008 *World Affairs* article entitled, "What Lies Beneath: Bush and Liberal Idealists," Kazin wrote:

> The phantom threat of Saddam Hussein's weapons of mass destruction, motivated the United States to invade and occupy Iraq. In March 2003, Deputy Defense Secretary Paul Wolfowitz promised the Veterans of Foreign

Wars that the imminent conflict "would be like wars that you've fought in, a war of liberation, a war to secure peace and freedom not only for ourselves, but for the Iraqi people who have suffered so long under one of the world's most brutal tyrannies." Two years later, George W. Bush declared, "Across the generations, we have proclaimed the imperative of self-government, because no one is fit to be a master, and no one deserves to be a slave." The president continued, "All who live in tyranny and hopelessness can know the United States will not ignore your oppression, or excuse your oppressors. When you stand for liberty, we will stand with you."

Kazin added, "There is nothing conservative about these statements."

Kazin is correct that Bush and other officials' statements reflected a progressive ideology and the author noted that "George W. Bush epitomizes the more aggressive side of this liberal tradition." In his book *The Last Best Hope: Restoring Conservatism and America's Promise*, MSNBC talk show host Joe Scarborough said of Republicans in 2007, "We've not been conservative as a party.... We have been radical," and asks, "Why did so few conservatives criticize Mr. Bush's Wilsonian pronouncement that the United States of America would lead a global democratic revolution that would end tyranny itself? What exactly were conservatives thinking during Mr. Bush's second inaugural address when the Republican president promised the world that U.S. troops would single-handedly bring freedom and peace to all corners of the globe?"

Sad to say, conservatives were not thinking. Government exploded and there was a not-so-coincidental correlation between an ambitious foreign policy and astronomical spending that too many conservatives were willing to ignore because they had adopted the same utopian vision as the philosophically liberal neoconservatives. The Tea Party is now a threat to the old Republican guard precisely because its stated principles prevent it from being brought into the neoconservative fold—Tea Partiers simply ask too many questions, and want to cut much more government than many in the party are going to be comfortable with.

Thanks to the Tea Party, the same name calling that led to my dad being unwelcome at the Republican National Convention in 2008 did not work when the same Republicans attempted to smear me in 2010. During my primary campaign, an aide to former Vice President Dick Cheney sent out a memo to other Republican establishment types declaring that I "held dangerous views on foreign policy." In a sense, Cheney's aide was right: My measured and conservative views on foreign policy, rooted in the Founding and informed by the Constitution, are indeed dangerous to neoconservative ideologues who are always anxious to find new excuses to get us involved in conflicts abroad.

This is not an exaggeration. There have been many mischaracterizations by neoconservatives of my or my father's foreign policy views—that in questioning government policy we are somehow "appeasing" the enemy or being anti-American. These detestable and genuinely anti-American attitudes more accurately belong to our critics, most of whom are always looking for a fight. One of the more disturbing examples of this was explained by Gen. Hugh Shelton in his book *Without Hesitation: The Odyssey of an American Warrior*, in which he describes how White House ideologues were itching for war with Iraq long before 9/11:

> "Hugh, I know I shouldn't even be asking you this, but what we really need in order to go in and take out Saddam is a precipitous event—something that would make us look good in the eyes of the world. Could you have one of our U-2s fly low enough—and slow enough—so as to guarantee that Saddam could shoot it down?" The hair on the back of my neck bristled, my teeth clenched, and my fists tightened. I was so mad I was about to explode. I looked across the table, thinking about the pilot in the U-2 and responded, "Of course we can..." which prompted a big smile on the official's face.
>
> "You can?" was the excited reply.
>
> "Why, of course we can," I countered. "Just as soon as we get your ass qualified to fly it, I will have it flown just as low and slow as you want to go."
>
> The official reeled back and immediately the smile disappeared. "I knew I should not have asked that...."
>
> "No, you should not have," I strongly agreed, still shocked at the disrespect and sheer audacity of the question. "Remember, there is one of our great Americans flying that U-2, and you are asking me to intentionally send him or her to their death for an opportunity to kick Saddam. The last time I checked, we don't operate like that here in America."

With an intimate knowledge of how deceptively our government can operate, General Shelton today calls the Iraq War "unnecessary," believes the Bush administration went to war "based on a series of lies," and says that "spinning the possible possession of WMDs as a threat to the United States in the way they did is, in my opinion, tantamount to intentionally deceiving the American people." Shelton's experience should serve as a lesson for conservatives, many of whom often confuse patriotism with simply accepting whatever the government tells them concerning foreign policy.

"Making the world safe for democracy" is not a proper American foreign policy, much less a conservative one.

Reagan Republicans?

It is not unusual for neoconservatives to invoke Reagan's legacy to justify their support for the Iraq war and other conflicts. Yet, judging the man by his actual policies and not the wild imaginations of some of his champions, it is quite hard to fathom Reagan invading Iraq under the same circumstances Bush did. Or as Colin Dueck, associate professor of public and international affairs at George Mason University and author of *Hard Line: The Republican Party and U.S. Foreign Policy since World War II*, explained in *RealClearPolitics*: "The United States did not embark on any large-scale or lasting military interventions under Reagan. He used force in a way that was brief, small-scale, and popular domestically, and when these conditions did not obtain, he extricated the U.S. from the possibility of protracted military entanglements."

Clearly, there is a distinct difference between military actions taken by Reagan, and the nation building advocated by today's neoconservatives. Writing for *Foreign Policy* magazine, journalist Peter Beinart gives a pretty good rundown of Reagan's actual foreign policy:

> Today's conservatives have conjured a mythic Reagan who never compromised with America's enemies and never shrank from a fight. But the real Reagan did both those things, often. In fact, they were a big part of his success.
>
> Sure, Reagan spent boatloads—some $2.8 trillion all told—on the military. And yes, he funneled money and guns to anti-communist rebels like the Nicaraguan Contras and Afghan mujahideen, while lecturing Soviet leader Mikhail Gorbachev to tear down that wall. But on the ultimate test of hawkdom—the willingness to send U.S. troops into harm's way—Reagan was no bird of prey. He launched exactly one land war, against Grenada, whose army totaled 600 men. It lasted two days. And his only air war—the 1986 bombing of Libya—was even briefer. Compare that with George H.W. Bush, who launched two midsized ground operations, in Panama (1989) and Somalia (1992), and one large war in the Persian Gulf (1991). Or with Bill Clinton, who launched three air campaigns—in Bosnia (1995), Iraq (1998), and Kosovo (1999)—each of which dwarfed Reagan's Libya bombing in duration and intensity. Do I even need to mention George W. Bush?

Many neoconservatives also criticized Reagan's diplomatic efforts concerning the Soviet Union. A common neoconservative tactic, also used in the build-up to the Iraq War, is to portray every new enemy on the horizon as the "next Hitler," any diplomatic efforts short of war as "appeasement," and to portray a war-reluctant America as taking the position of British Prime Minister Neville Chamberlain when he signed a peace treaty with Germany in 1939. Reagan's cautious foreign policy approach was attacked on similar grounds by the same reflexively militaristic neoconservatives, particularly Norman Podhoretz, a leading neoconservative intellectual. Wrote Fredrik Logevall and Kenneth Osgood in *World Affairs*: "As early as 1983, when Reagan was embarking on the largest peacetime military buildup in U.S. history, Norman Podhoretz compared Reagan to Chamberlain and complained that 'appeasement by any other name smells as rank, and the stench of it now pervades the American political atmosphere.' Reagan had become a 'Carter clone,' Podhoretz later griped, warning—less than two years before the fall of the Berlin Wall—that 'the danger is greater than ever.'"

In retrospect, what was a better approach to the Soviet Union: Reagan's diplomacy, which eventually led to the end of the Cold War and the Soviet Union itself, or the neoconservative approach, which might have prolonged the Cold War and feasibly led to a hot one?

It's worth mentioning that many conservative Republicans during the late 1990s opposed Clinton's foreign interventions. Conservative talk host Sean Hannity's description of the Clinton administration's actions in Kosovo reflected Republican thinking at the time and could just as easily be applied to President Obama's escalation in Afghanistan today: "It seems that we're talking about a very ill-conceived military action here. And now the question is, do you go in further and deeper, or do you pull back and rethink what the strategy's going to be here, because there has really been no stated goal, mission, or objective.... There's no definition of success. All these important things. There's no exit strategy. One mistake after another. Why would you go in deeper when we have not been successful up to this point? That seems to me to be folly."

When George W. Bush ran for president in 2000, he criticized much of Clinton's foreign interventionism and nation-building efforts, and his rhetoric reflected conservative sentiment within the Republican Party at that time. Said Bush during a 2000 debate with Vice President Al Gore: "I'm not so sure the role of the United States is to go around the world and say, 'This is the way it's got to be.'...I think one way for us to end up being viewed as the 'ugly American' is for us to go around the world saying, 'We do it this way, so should you." Criticizing Clinton's decision to intervene in Somalia, Bush said, "I don't think our troops ought to be used for what's called 'nation building.'" When asked how people around the world should view America, Bush said, "It really depends upon how our nation conducts its foreign policy. If we're an arrogant nation, they'll resent us. If we're a humble nation, they'll respect us."

Not surprisingly, the neoconservatives sided with the Clinton administration in the 1990s and against much of the Republican Party, as these same Republican hawks support Obama's troop escalation in Afghanistan today. Meanwhile, conservatives such as Glenn Beck, Joe Scarborough, George Will, Tony Blankley, Ann Coulter—and even Republican National Committee Chairman Michael Steele—have questioned the wisdom of our current president's war of "necessity."

Asking such questions was also a hallmark of Reagan's presidency, and perhaps the best comparative description of Reagan's cautioned, contemplative and more traditionally conservative approach to foreign policy, was best explained by

David Keene, chairman of the American Conservative Union: "(Reagan) resorted to military force far less often than many of those who came before him or who have since occupied the Oval Office.... After the (1983) assault on the Marine barracks in Lebanon, it was questioning the wisdom of U.S. involvement that led Reagan to withdraw our troops rather than dig in. He found no good strategic reason to give our regional enemies inviting U.S. targets."

Keene added, "Can one imagine one of today's neoconservative absolutists backing away from any fight anywhere?"

Keene's recollection of Reagan and his foreign policy is instructive, and though every Republican likes to claim the mantle of Ronald Reagan these days, some should at least study his actual record before making such claims.

Fighting Radical Islam Does Not Require Foreign Aid and Nation Building

The Right's embrace of nation-building during the Bush years was perplexing. When the government announces a massive effort at social transformation, you expect conservatives to be the leading skeptics.
    Gene Healey, Vice President, Cato Institute

Given the gravity of our wars in Iraq and Afghanistan, there are many basic logistic and commonsense questions that should be asked but rarely are. For example, in fighting terrorist organizations, members of which can be found in numerous different countries, does it make sense to invade and occupy a nation for years or decades? Would a war on street gangs in which police invaded and occupied Chicago be effective in getting rid of street gangs nationwide? How about the fact that before we went to war with Iraq there had never been any Al-Qaeda or even a suicide bomber in the history of that country? After we invaded, this was no longer the case. What developments have occurred in Iraq since the war began that might further prevent terrorist attacks? What are we currently doing in Afghanistan that could possibly prevent another underwear bomber or Times Square terrorist? How does permanent occupation and nation building in the Middle East do anything to stop such acts? Or perhaps worse—does permanent occupation and nation building encourage terrorists?

Conservatives rightly understand that government intervention at home—from taxation to pat-downs in airports by TSA workers—affects citizens' behavior in multiple ways. Is it possible that decades of arguably far more intrusive behavior by the United States in Islamic nations has also had an effect on those populations, encouraging and increasing the threat of Islamic terrorism? The CIA created the term *blowback* to describe this phenomenon and the 9/11 Commission Report cites blowback as a primary cause of the September 11, 2001 attacks. The standard neoconservative line throughout the Iraq and Afghanistan wars has been that America must "fight terrorists over there so we don't have to fight them here," but former head of the CIA's Bin Laden Unit, terrorism expert Michael Scheuer, stresses that they come here precisely because we are over there. Writes Scheuer: "On no other foreign policy issue since the Cold War's end has the truth been so easy to establish on the basis of hard facts but so hard for Americans to see...that Muslim hatred is motivated by U.S. interventionism more than any other factor."

Many like to claim that Muslim hatred for our culture or "our freedom," to use Bush's language, is what causes Islamic terrorism. This is likely a factor in terrorists' efforts and recruitment, but not the primary factor, or as Scheuer says bluntly: "We are at war because of what the U.S. government does in the Muslim world—unqualified support for Israel, support for Arab tyrannies, invading Iraq, etc.—and not for who we are and how we live here in North America." If Scheuer was wrong, or the CIA really had no justification for developing the term *blowback*, and it really was Americans' way of life that was a primary factor for Islamic terrorist attacks—logic would follow that more culturally liberal nations like Sweden or Switzerland would have more to fear from radical Islam than the United States.

It also would be a mistake to blame such terrorism purely on Islamic ideology. Consider this: Has Islam changed much since the 1940s, 1950s and 1960s when there was virtually no Islamic terrorist threat to the United States? Has America's involvement and policies toward the Middle East changed significantly since that time? Writes the Cato Institute's Robert Pape:

> Al Qaeda is a paradoxical entity: a group with territorial concerns but no territory of its own. It came about in response to the presence of thousands of American troops on the Arabian Peninsula after 1990, and recruited terrorists for suicide missions with the primary aim of forcing them out. Though it speaks of Americans as infidels, al Qaeda is less concerned with converting us to Islam than removing us from Arab and Muslim lands, and it was in this cause that it attacked our embassies in

Kenya and Tanzania in 1998, the U.S.S. *Cole* in 2000, and the World Trade Center and Pentagon on 9/11.

If US occupation is a primary recruitment tool and what inspires Islamic terrorists, are many of our current efforts overseas actually fighting terrorism and diminishing the threat? Or does our being involved in nation building possibly increase the threat? Pape continues:

> From 2002 to the end of 2005, al Qaeda carried out over 17 suicide and other terrorist bombings, killing nearly 700 people—more attacks and victims than in all the years before 9/11 combined. Most Americans would like to believe that Western counter-terrorism efforts have weakened al Qaeda, but by the measure that counts—the ability of the group to kill us—it is stronger today than it was before 9/11.... We must understand that suicide terrorism results more from foreign occupation than Islamic fundamentalism, and conduct the war accordingly.

On the campaign trail I met Dan Ballou, a circuit judge who is also a proud Marine. You would likely not meet a more patriotic American, but he was galled by what he was asked to do in Afghanistan. He was told by his superiors to supervise the buying of weapons from the Taliban. He objected for two reasons: one, how do we trust that this money does not end up buying IEDs (improvised explosive devices) that wound and maim us tomorrow? And two, I'm a Marine! I was trained to take weapons from America's enemies, not buy them!

CBS ran a story during the campaign alleging that a significant portion of the $2.16 billion in American taxpayer dollars used for rebuilding efforts in Afghanistan were funneled to the Taliban as protection money. Reported CBS News' Lara Logan, "Billions of U.S. taxpayer dollars are fueling corruption in Afghanistan and funding the insurgency, according to a six-month investigation by the House Subcommittee on National Security and Foreign Affairs. That would mean that the U.S. is literally funding the enemy, as violence escalates daily in Afghanistan and more U.S. soldiers and Marines are dying than ever before in this war."

Our GIs don't get this and don't like it. I met with a platoon leaving from Fort Knox. It was an impromptu gathering in which our campaign was having a separate event at the same restaurant. A couple of the GIs recognized me and came over. They said they were fans of my father's and me as well. (What fascinated and perplexed the neocons was that Ron Paul, who campaigned against the Iraq War and campaigned for only going to war with a formal constitutional declaration, ended up with more contributions from soldiers than any other presidential candidate). The GIs asked if I would come next door and speak to the group that was leaving for Afghanistan. I was thrilled at the prospect. I had no prepared speech so I simply said:

I am proud of you for your willingness to defend our country, to defend our freedom. I know that you don't get to make policy. The nature of the military is that you take commands. But I am a civilian and I want to be one of those who does make policy, who decides when and where or if you have to go into harm's way. I tell you, if I'm elected, I will treat that decision with the utmost respect. I would only vote to send you to battle as if I were sending one of my sons. America is and should be reluctant to go to war. When we go to war, we must declare it formally as the Constitution requires."

I then added: "I know you don't get to make policy but I want to know your opinion. I want to know your opinion more than anyone else's because you have volunteered to fight for your country. The question I ask you is, are the Afghans doing enough? After ten years of war, are the Afghans doing enough? Should they be patrolling the streets in these remote villages? Raise your hand if you think we are not turning over the control to the Afghans fast enough?"

The vast majority of these brave young men and women raised their hands. They will do their patriotic duty as commanded but they also want the Afghans to step up and, after ten years, most of these soldiers wondered why the Afghans can't shoulder more of the burden.

Obama's former National Security Adviser Jim Jones said that there are less than 100 Al-Qaeda members in Afghanistan. Do we need 100,000 soldiers to combat 100 Al-Qaeda? Bruce Fein, author and former assistant attorney general under Reagan, has made the case that if the United States took the troop-to-enemy ratio currently in the Middle East and applied it to World War II, America would have stationed three billion soldiers in Europe alone, ten times the size of the current U.S. population. As for the often impossible situations in which we so readily and regularly place our soldiers, is it appropriate for US tax dollars to be paid to the Taliban to ask them not to fight? That's exactly what's happening. While building schools in Afghanistan, US contractors have to pay the Taliban protection money so that they don't attack them. The

Taliban reportedly takes such funds and sets IEDs to harm or kill our soldiers, indirectly from U.S. taxpayer money. This is the insanity of nation building.

Last year, when Republican National Committee Chairman Michael Steele dared to question Obama's wisdom in fighting a land war in Afghanistan, he was attacked by many in the GOP—most of them members of the Republican establishment—for daring to even ask the question. Calling for Steele's resignation, *Weekly Standard* editor William Kristol wrote, "There are, of course, those who think we should pull out of Afghanistan, and they're certainly entitled to make their case. But one of them shouldn't be the chairman of the Republican party."

I beg to differ. Why is it acceptable for Republicans to question Obama about healthcare, climate change, stimulus, immigration, financial overhaul, and pretty much anything else, but when it comes to probably the most important decision we ever have to make—the decision to wage war—questioning foreign policy is completely off-limits?

Given the great sacrifice we ask of our soldiers, combined with our monstrous debt, is it not imperative that we ask these questions? Post-Bush, it's encouraging to see more conservatives doing just this. Columnist George Will has described the foolishness of the nation building in Afghanistan: "Nation-building would be impossible even if we knew how.... If U.S. forces are there to prevent reestablishment of Al Qaeda bases—evidently there are none now—must there be nation-building invasions of Somalia, Yemen, and other sovereignty vacuums?" Will also notes the dismal logistics: "U.S. forces are being increased by 21,000, to 68,000, bringing the coalition total to 110,000.... Counterinsurgency theory concerning the time and the ratio of forces required to protect the population indicates that, nationwide, Afghanistan would need hundreds of thousands of coalition troops, perhaps for a decade or more. That is inconceivable."

In defending Steele, pundit Ann Coulter wrote in her syndicated column, "Republicans used to think seriously about deploying the military. President Eisenhower sent aid to South Vietnam, but said he could not 'conceive of a greater tragedy' for America than getting heavily involved there." Coulter would add in response to Kristol's attacks on Steele, "I thought the irreducible requirements of Republicanism were being for life, small government and a strong national defense, but I guess permanent war is on the platter now, too."

That Coulter makes a distinction between a "strong national defense" and "permanent war" is important, because too often we tend to confuse the two. I would argue that most of what we do around the world has little to do with actual "defense" in much the same way welfare has little to do with actually helping the poor. If you look at the history of welfare in America, you will find that we have mostly subsidized the problem of poverty, creating generations now dependent on the government. If you look at much of the history of our foreign policy, in which we've often tried to be the policeman of the world, you will find that we've subsidized much of the globe with foreign and military aid, little of which has anything to do with our actual national security and all of which we can no longer afford.

In my proposals to end foreign aid, many critics often ask, "Well what about our ally Israel?" Actually, Israel's example illustrates the problem. We give about $4 billion annually to Israel in foreign aid—and we give about $6 billion to the nations that surround Israel, many of them antagonistic toward the Jewish state. Does this make any sense at all? Does any of this have actually anything to do with America's national security, much less Israel's? Who truly benefits from the United States funding both sides of such an arms race?

Yet we've been doing this for decades with little to no questions asked, because it's become an entrenched part of our politics. It is this sort of mindless, status quo politics, both foreign and abroad, that prevents us from trying new, more productive ideas or applying fresh approaches to the same old problems. George Will describes well this self-defeating mentality as it relates to our war in Afghanistan: "Those Americans who say Afghanistan is a test of America's 'staying power' are saying we must stay there because we are there. This is steady work, but treats perseverance as a virtue regardless of context or consequences, and makes futility into a reason for persevering."

In the name of keeping us safe, both fiscally and physically, our foreign interventionism must be lessened and foreign aid must end so that our form of representative democracy can endure—a model of government best exported by example, not by force, and certainly never at our own expense.

Fighting an Unconventional War

[The New Hampshire Tea Party founder's] hope is that there will be a "group of people coming out of Iraq and Afghanistan that knows—knows what the military can do and can't do." One of his sons had been in Afghanistan. When the son came home and saw the Tea Party protests

he said, "Here we are fighting a huge central government.
And what are we trying to impose on Afghanistan?"
"The Tea Party's Foreign Policy," P. J. O'Rourke,
World Affairs, September/October 2010

In any war we fight, we must always go reluctantly and con-stitutionally, though America hasn't officially declared war since World War II. War is a horrible but sometimes necessary endeavor. If it is a soldier's job to do his duty, it should be the citizens' job to make sure that every time their government sends our bravest men and women off to fight, it's for a good reason. Not questioning our government on these matters does a disservice to our military, and I will only vote to go to war through a declaration of war, as the Founders intended and our soldiers deserve.

Yet it must be said that victory in the war on Islamic ter-rorism will not come in solving others' problems throughout the world, but attempting to practically solve our own. Nor will there ever be a complete "victory." Terrorism is a tactic and therefore someone, somewhere, will always attempt to use it. The notion that government must, or can, create a risk-free environment is not only impossible, but antithetical to the very concept of a free society. After 9/11, the government's reaction was to federalize airport security and institute what some would consider Draconian search and pat-down mea-sures. After 9/11, my father's first proposals included intro-ducing language into a bill that would put a moratorium on student visas for about ten countries that were associated with terrorism. But this proposal never took hold. My father says even the Bush administration was opposed to his moratorium proposal. I guess some believe it is better to search millions of Americans at the airports than to institute some targeted police work to identify those who might come to attack us.

After 9/11 Ron Paul also introduced the "Air Piracy and Reprisal Act of 2001" and the "September 11 Marque and Reprisal Act of 2001," both based in Article 1, Section 8 of the Constitution, which states that Congress has the authority to "declare War, grant Letters of Marque and Reprisal, and make Rules concerning Captures on Land and Water." The concept of marque and reprisal is something President Jefferson had used to fight Barbary pirates in 1801. My father's idea was in recognizing that an outfit like Al-Qaeda cannot be fought in a conventional war—or by invading and occupying nations. Congress could raise money to pay private individuals or contractors to arrest or eliminate individual terrorists. This is probably not a perfect method, and perhaps military black-ops or other methods could also be effective, but the point is that focusing on the actual terrorists instead of waging conventional wars might produce better results. These ideas would have also been much less costly, in lives and dollars.

Before further interrogating our children or grandparents at the airport, perhaps the federal government might want to finally get serious about securing our borders, where Al-Qaeda members could feasibly waltz into the United States any time they like. After 9/11, it is telling that our federal government's first impulse was to further intrude into the lives of private citizens—whether through the PATRIOT Act or the proposed "REAL ID," national identification proposal that thankfully never took hold—before trying to get a handle on the millions of non-citizens currently residing in the United States. Similar to my father's proposal after 9/11, I've proposed that we better regulate and limit the number of visas we accept from questionable nations from which Islamic terrorists have previously emanated. Months after the 9/11 attacks, some of the dead nineteen hijackers were even reissued their student visas. This sort of government incompetence must end.

America needs a strong national defense—but how do we best defend ourselves? The old methods of invading and occupying foreign nations do little to prevent a lone individual or collection of individuals, sometimes even from the United States, from attempting to carry out a terrorist attack. These wars also do much to encourage such actions, both home and abroad. An unconventional war will require unconventional approaches coupled with a return to common sense—and a recognition that the old foreign policy status quo simply will not do.

For a nation as rich and as powerful as ours, there is no reason why we can't have the strongest military on earth that operates within our budget and the confines of the Constitution and, perhaps most important, only in our legitimate interests and defense. To do otherwise is unreasonable, unproductive and unconscionable.

And unaffordable.

8

★ ★ ★

The Perils of Government Intervention

There is only one difference between a bad economist and a good one: the bad economist confines himself to the visible effect; the good economist takes into account both the effect that can be seen and those effects that must be foreseen.

Frédéric Bastiat

The less government we have the better.

Ralph Waldo Emerson

Government intervention almost always leads to unintended consequences. This has certainly been true of American foreign policy.

For example, today we must constantly guard against radical Islam but throughout the 1980s it was the official policy of the State Department to encourage radical jihad in Afghanistan. When Osama bin Laden claimed that it was American troops or "infidels" stationed on the Arabian Peninsula, or "holy land," that inspired him to plot 9/11, he was using the same reasoning our CIA once encouraged when we were trying to undermine the Soviets. Eight years ago we went to war in Iraq, but throughout the 1980s we sent billions of dollars and allegedly even chemical weapons to Saddam Hussein, in an effort to contain Iran. When our government warned that Hussein might possess chemical weapons, you could say we were acting on "inside information." Today we are told we must be concerned about a more powerful Iran which, of course, has only become an issue since we defeated their archenemy, Iraq.

Many might say that we had to encourage radical jihad in Afghanistan to contain the Soviet Union, or that we had to go to war with Iraq because we had to "do something," given the gravity of the threats we faced. Continuing in this vein, today President Obama has authorized drone strikes in Pakistan that some military experts say create more terrorists than they kill, which, if true, makes the "war on terror" more a war for it.

Perhaps some of these government interventions overseas, from the 1980s to today, were necessary. Perhaps some were not. What can't be denied is that they created unintended consequences and, in some cases, those consequences might have been worse than the initial problems our interventions were supposed to solve.

Such is the nature of government, which is precisely why the Founders viewed military use, even when warranted, as something that should be definite and limited. George Washington told us: "Government is not reason; it is not eloquence; it is force. . . . Never for a moment should it be left to irresponsible action." Science tells us that for every action there is an equal and opposite reaction. Yet today it seems we are much less hesitant to use government action, whether abroad or domestically, than the Founders could have ever imagined. The Founding Fathers also would not be surprised to see that trying to solve problems with continuous government action creates its own set of problems. Not surprisingly, the majority of what our federal government does today, abroad or domestically, also continues to take place well outside the parameters of the Constitution.

Some like to say that operating within the confines of the Constitution is impossible in today's modern world. They say that in this age of global threats, global economies and technological progress, America's founding document has simply become a relic. They say that a charter written by men who wore powdered wigs and traveled by horse and buggy has no bearing on the modern United States.

I beg to differ. The genius of the Founders was that they had studied history, particularly that of ancient Greece and Rome, and had determined that man was fallible in any age. The Constitution was designed precisely to limit men, particularly powerful men, who might use the instrument of government to do harm even in the name of doing good. Jefferson believed that "In questions of power...let no more be heard of confidence in man, but bind him down from mischief by the chains of the Constitution." We all know how the path to hell was paved, and today we should recognize just how much damage our government causes in the name of good intentions.

Every problem on the horizon does not require a government solution; and if we were to follow the Constitution again, we might rediscover exactly why the Founders feared— and attempted to restrain—runaway government.

Every time we face a problem, someone somewhere declares that government must "do something."

No, it mustn't.

What If We Did Nothing?

We have much more to fear in this town from hasty than from slow government action.
George F. Will

The very notion that government must always "do something" is not only exactly what the Founders wanted to prevent, but often leads critics of the Tea Party to suggest that the movement is all complaints and no solutions. This misperception is based on a flawed premise. The Tea Party's message reflects Reagan's axiom that government is the problem. Spending, debt, high taxes, burdensome regulation—these are the problems the Tea Party now targets and all are almost entirely created by a "helpful" government trying to find "solutions."

One solution I have suggested is that the Senate should wait one day for every twenty pages of new legislation that is proposed. This would give senators time to actually read bills before passing them—a rarity on Capitol Hill these days—and would slow down the rush for more government. Naturally, many of my critics say that this isn't really a solution to our problems, but it is—once one recognizes that government has been the problem. Given their view of government, I'm not surprised that many don't agree with me, just as I'm not surprised by their continued criticism of me and the Tea Party.

When the Tea Party has flexed its political muscle to unseat politicians who supported TARP or voted for federal stimulus, a popular establishment response has been, "Imagine if we did nothing?" Yes, let's imagine this. In 2008, when the federal government was offering a $700 billion stimulus and the Fed was once again artificially lowering interest rates, FOX News' Neil Cavuto wrote:

> On a day we did everything to help the markets: A question. What if we did nothing? If we offered no stimulus to calm them down? Cut not a single interest rate to calm them down? Did not a thing to calm them down. Nothing at all. What if we let markets be markets and tumble on their own? And recover on their own? What if

we didn't cede to their tantrums and ignored their tantrums? Very smart folks say a lot of not so very smart folks would get burned. Cruel thing sometimes, these markets. Crueler yet to extend that agony or delay that agony.

Cavuto makes a good point. Delaying the agony of failing banks on the backs of taxpayers is not only unfair to the taxpayer but a negation of the free market, in which government privatizes corporate profits but socializes the losses. Despite what the many "smart folks" or "experts" tell us, doing nothing would have actually been the preferable course, a point commentator Álvaro Vargas Llosa also made during the bank bailouts at *RealClearPolitics* in a column entitled "Let Those Banks Fail!":

Few things give a worse name to the free-enterprise system than offloading bank losses onto taxpayers. The way to solve this crisis is to let "zombie" banks proceed to their beyond, allowing those banks that need restructuring to start doing just that while those in a position to fill the space left by failed institutions can jump in quickly. After all, a majority of the almost 9,000 U.S. banks, including regional institutions, did not engage in credit hanky-panky and would love a chance to increase their market share.

Llosa added: "It is common knowledge that for years, Americans have lived beyond their means by saving too little and borrowing too much. If this is readily accepted, why is it so difficult to see that a government-induced expansion of credit at a time when American households are finally trying to pay back their debts and save for the future will only prolong the problem?"

With freedom comes responsibility and sometimes individuals don't always make the right choices. When they don't, they pay the price, learn their lesson, and move on, better educated, situated and solvent.

The same is true of free markets.

Even in the name of "protecting" the American people, government intervention tends to become costly very quickly. When President Bush declared that he'd "abandoned free-market principles to save the free-market system" during the bank bailouts, he neglected to mention that it was precisely government intervention in the free market that had led to the financial crisis. Many on the Left, including liberal documentarian Michael Moore, have done a good job of outlining how things went south, who benefited and who got hurt, but always blame the free market for the crisis while simultaneously insisting the government must do more. But it was precisely because the government did too much that we had a financial crisis—and doing more could feasibly make our nation's condition even more critical.

How Government Intervention Caused the Financial Crisis

Where did all the excess, risk, leverage, and debt, not to mention the housing bubble itself, come from? When questions like this are raised, the answers are, to say the least, unhelpful. "Excessive risk-taking" simply begs the question. As several economists have noted, blaming the crisis on "greed" is like blaming plane crashes on gravity.

Thomas E. Woods Jr., *Meltdown*

In 2009, talk show host Glenn Beck began promoting something he called the "9/12 Project," designed to bring Americans back to the unity and purpose many felt on the day after 9/11. Inspired by Beck, groups had formed that were similar to the Tea Party in that they were locally organized and barely had any association with 9/12 groups in other cities. Not surprisingly, many of the 9/12 folks are Tea Partiers and vice versa, and share the same concerns about where the country is headed.

In spring 2009, after a full day of seeing patients, I drove two hours to Danville, Kentucky, to speak to the local 9/12 Project. During my speech, I looked at the wealthiest man in the crowd and said, "It's greed if it's your money. If it's my money, it's self-interest." Everyone laughed. I explained that (much like calling someone "racist" or "isolationist") the oft-used pejorative "greedy" is just another example of name calling—and was the logical fallacy ad hominem.

It was during the credit crisis in the fall of 2007 that everyone was declaring that "greed" and "stupidity" had caused the crisis, and I immediately knew that if this explanation took hold it would simply be another indirect, misplaced attack on capitalism and free markets. During the presidential election, both Obama and McCain decried the "greed" of Wall Street and blamed "greed" for the mortgage crisis. *New York Times* columnist David Brooks wrote: "The greed narrative leads to the conclusion that government should aggressively restructure the financial sector." By accepting this "greed narrative" as the cause of the crisis and great recession, we would implicitly be accepting that capitalism had failed and that the motivating factor, the "invisible hand" that guides the marketplace—self-interest—was at fault.

But how did everyone become greedy at the same time, just all of a sudden? How did virtually everyone in one particular industry—the mortgage industry—become greedy and stupid, all at the same time? The very notion is absurd. It wasn't that all of mankind had all of a sudden embraced one of the seven deadly sins in one fell swoop.

Michael S. Rozeff, a retired professor of finance, has pointed out that this could only happen if some signal was sent to everyone simultaneously—to virtually every actor throughout the economy—that it had become profitable to sell houses to people who had little to no down payment.

The universal "signal" that created havoc was when the Federal Reserve lowered interest rates significantly below what the market dictated, and continued to do this for several years. These artificially low rates sent a signal to builders, borrowers and lenders to just keep on truckin'—which led to profound inflation in housing prices. From the Great Depression to 2003 the median price of a house had gradually increased. Or seen from another vantage point, the value of the dollar had steadily declined for most of the twentieth century. Did mortgage bankers just suddenly become stupid over the next four years? Or were they basing their decisions on information supplied by bad government policy?

The mortgage crisis played out along the lines of what Austrian economists call a "boom-bust cycle." To discover what caused a "bust," or correction, in the marketplace you must first discover the cause of the "boom." The housing sector boomed for at least a decade and home prices doubled and sometimes tripled because the Federal Reserve had manipulated the interest rate. Greenspan relentlessly lowered interest rates to "stimulate the economy," intervening in the wake of the dot-com crisis of 2001.

The median home price had risen consistently since the Depression but the slope of the home price curve began to grow exponentially after 2001. As the median price of homes soared, mortgage companies became aware that potential owners with little or no down payment could "gain" equity simply by buying the $120,000 house with nothing down because the value of the home would magically increase to, say, $160,000 within a year or two. The homeowner with no down payment now had "equity" in his home without a down payment. The lender might then say, "Congratulations, you now have $20,000 in equity. Would you like to put in a swimming pool?"

This scenario works only so long as homes' median price rises. Riskier sub-primes would remain profitable only if the average value of homes continued to rise on a steep curve. The government promoted these subprime loans designed to make homeowners out of people who didn't have down payments. The Bush administration bragged that over a million new homeowners were created by these policies. These homeowners became the sub-prime market.

Tax code changes eliminated the deductibility of many forms of debt other than home mortgages and second mortgages (equity loans), thereby further accelerating the mortgage boom. What caused the meltdown? In 2006, for the first time since the Great Depression, the median price of homes fell. The riskier loans depended on a continued rise in the home prices. Why did the price trend change? Like any product where costs are kept artificially low, the artificially low interest rates ultimately caused an oversupply of homes.

In retrospect, should the mortgage lenders and the banks that bought and sold these mortgages have known better? Perhaps. But an entire sector of the economy can only be led into bad decision-making by some uniform or systemic misinformation. The Federal Reserve creates money and manipulates the interest rates. By keeping interest rates artificially low, the Federal Reserve created the boom and disseminated bad information to the marketplace. Thousands of mortgage brokers and bankers acted on that knowledge with the intention of making money—not because they suddenly became greedy—but because they are, as all businesspeople are, seeking profit.

When the Federal Reserve creates credit or new money, it does so to pay for the federal deficit. You know—the deficit that grew $4 trillion dollars under a Republican president and a Republican Congress? This new money causes inflation or a rise in prices. Inflation does not always affect all prices equally. Over the past decade, inflation was concentrated largely in home prices and energy prices.

If we are to blame someone for the present financial crisis, perhaps it should be a profligate Congress that never met a spending bill it didn't like. Self-interest is not a bad thing. Self-interested entrepreneurs seek profit, that profit motive drives efficiency, and the resulting competition distributes goods to all of us. If you don't believe me, go to Wal-Mart and check out the cell phones available for $14.99.

Leaders of either party who blame the financial crisis on

"greed" are either deflecting blame from themselves, or else they simply don't know what they're talking about.

Many of the criticisms also continue to blame the free market and demand more government intervention, ignoring the fact that too much government intervention was a primary culprit. One such book, Charles R. Morris' *The Trillion Dollar Meltdown: Easy Money, High Rollers, and the Great Credit Crash*, argues that we need more government intervention to ensure another financial crisis doesn't occur. Morris seems to believe that the free market simply can't be left to its own devices, when in reality it's overregulated already. Reviewing Morris' book, Michael S. Rozeff writes:

> Our financial markets are anything but free. Bond raters have a quasi-cartel. Banks and insurers are heavily regulated. Money is monopolized by the Fed. Institutional investors who are legally separated from their contributors feel free to experiment with hedge funds. Accounting, under the aegis of the SEC and acting in a quasi-governmental way, does not keep up with innovative players. Like most "mainstream" commentators, however, Morris insists that the financial debacle is the fault of our mythical free market....If markets were free, financial players wouldn't be lavishing huge campaign contributions on congressmen in key positions. If markets were free, there would be no Fannie Mae and Freddie Mac sopping up mortgages across the nation, while repackaging and reselling them to institutional investors worldwide. If markets were free, Fannie Mae and Freddie Mac would not be in receivership.

In his mea culpa to Congress, former Federal Reserve chairman Alan Greenspan bailed on capitalism and blamed the crisis on his over-confidence in the marketplace—not his over-manipulation of interest rates. Greenspan opined that no one could have seen this coming.

Tell that to Michael J. Burry. He does not claim to have some supernatural ability to predict the future, but he made a fortune by recognizing the coming collapse in the home mortgage market. He explained that when he saw banks writing mortgages that were interest-only he knew the end was near. In a 2010 *New York Times* op-ed entitled "I Saw the Crisis Coming, Why Didn't the Fed?" Burry wrote:

> Alan Greenspan, the former chairman of the Federal Reserve, proclaimed last month that no one could have predicted the housing bubble. "Everybody missed it," he said, "academia, the Federal Reserve, all regulators." But that is not how I remember it. Back in 2005 and 2006, I argued as forcefully as I could, in letters to clients of my investment firm, Scion Capital, that the mortgage market would melt down in the second half of 2007, causing substantial damage to the economy....As a nation, we cannot afford to live with Mr. Greenspan's way of thinking....[T]he signs were all there in 2005, when a bursting of the bubble would have had far less dire consequences, and when the government could have acted to minimize the fallout. Instead, our leaders in Washington either willfully or ignorantly aided and abetted the bubble. And even when the full extent of the financial crisis became painfully clear early in 2007, the Federal Reserve

chairman, the Treasury secretary, the president and senior members of Congress repeatedly underestimated the severity of the problem, ultimately leaving themselves with only one policy tool—the epic and unfair taxpayer-financed bailouts.

Burry added: "It did not have to be this way. And at this point there is no reason to reflexively dismiss the analysis of those who foresaw the crisis."

Like Burry, Euro Pacific Capital President Peter Schiff was also dismissed in his economic analysis and predictions. When economist Arthur Laffer said in 2006, "The United States economy has never been in better shape. There is no tax increase coming in the next couple of years. Monetary policy is spectacular. We have freer trade than ever before." Schiff appeared on CNBC, responding:

It is going to be pretty bad and whether it starts in '07 or '08, I think is immaterial and I also think it is going to last not just for quarters but for years. See, the basic problem with the US economy is we have too much consumption and borrowing and not enough production and savings.... It is not wealth that has increased in the last few years; we haven't increased our productive capacity. All that has increased is the paper values of our stocks and real estate, but that's not real wealth any more than the NASDAQ was wealth. If you see the stock market come down and the real estate bubble burst, all that phony wealth is going to evaporate and all that is going to be left is all the debt we accumulated to foreigners.

Schiff's warnings were dismissed by virtually every "expert"—that is, until his predictions became reality. *Yahoo! Finance* reported in 2008: "There's a popular YouTube clip called 'Peter Schiff Was Right' that shows the president of Euro Pacific Capital engaged in on-air debates with financial luminaries such as Art Laffer and Ben Stein, circa 2006–07. The clips show the wisdom of Schiff's dire forecasts—and, judging from the dismissive reactions, just how far he was outside the mainstream."

Outside the mainstream? That's a badge of honor considering it was only those "outside the mainstream" who predicted the financial crisis.

"It's No Accident That Austrian Economics Is Newly Popular"

Austrian economists believe that low interest rates reflect wealth and savings and to lower them artificially projects a false reality that can lead to malinvestment and economic havoc. Does this not describe the housing bubble? The "mainstream" view, or Keynesian view (named for economist John Maynard Keynes, considered by many to be the father of modern economics), is that the more credit the better even if created through government manipulation of markets. Does this not also describe the housing bubble? This is nothing new. Libertarian journalist and famous New Deal critic Garet Garrett wrote of the Great Depression, in his 1932 book *A Bubble That Broke the World*: "From the beginning of economic thought it had been supposed that prosperity was from the increase and exchange of wealth, and credit was its product."

The Austrian School has had a resurgence of late, primarily because it has been right where so many mainstream economists have been wrong. You simply can't spend or borrow your way out of a recession, much less into prosperity. I have said repeatedly that if we don't stop our government's reckless behavior it will inevitably lead to a "day of reckoning." A Bloomberg.com article in November entitled "Irish Relief Fleeting as 'Day of Reckoning' Nears," demonstrated how Ireland's economic recklessness was already catching up with it:

> Borrowing costs for Europe's most indebted nations are at record highs as Ireland's capitulation in accepting a bailout of its banking industry stokes concern that other countries also will have to seek aid.... "It's no longer taboo to speak about a restructuring," said Johannes Jooste, a portfolio strategist at Bank of America Corp.'s Merrill Lynch Global Wealth Management in London, which oversees about $1.4 trillion for clients. "The fact that bond yields continue to rise and put pressure on countries that have to fund from the market makes investors less and less confident, and it's bringing forward the day of reckoning."

Like Greece in 2009 and our country under Obama, Ireland's government officials were looking to be bailed out: "While Ireland has enough money to pay its debts until the middle of next year, it has requested a bailout from the European Union and International Monetary Fund amid concern the cost of rescuing its banks would overwhelm government finances."

Bailouts don't work, they only prolong the problem. Iceland's refusal to bail out its banks is a good example of this. In November a Bloomberg.com headline read "Iceland Is No Ireland as State Free of Bank Debt." Reported Bloomberg.com:

> Iceland's President Olafur R. Grimsson said his country is better off than Ireland thanks to the government's decision to allow the banks to fail two years ago and because the krona (Icelandic currency) could be devalued. "The difference is that in Iceland we allowed the banks to fail," Grimsson said in an interview with Bloomberg Television's Mark Barton today. "These were private banks and we didn't pump money into them in order to keep them going; the state did not shoulder the responsibility of the failed private banks."

Grimsson would add: "How far can we ask ordinary people—farmers and fishermen and teachers and doctors and nurses—to shoulder the responsibility of failed private banks...? Iceland is faring much better than anybody expected...." Once again, Austrian economists could have predicted this. CNBC's John Carney writes that Austrian economics "provides the best explanation for the business cycle we just lived through.... I think that we may have entered a new era.... Not since the New Deal has Austrian economics enjoyed the political popularity it does now [particularly with] the Republican Party, especially its Tea Party wing. Peter Schiff, the Austrian economics–inflected investment advisor, is a very popular guest on business television. Tom Woods's book *Meltdown*—which provided an Austrian economics explanation for the financial crisis—was a best seller. Congressman Ron Paul and Senator-elect Rand Paul are both devotees."

Woods' book *Meltdown: A Free-Market Look at Why the Stock Market Collapsed, the Economy Tanked and Government Bailouts Will Make Things Worse* is one of the best explanations of the financial crisis from the Austrian perspective. Woods focuses on the Federal Reserve's role in creating the 2007 financial crisis and why the Fed's policy of "quantitative easing"—or printing new money out of thin air—doesn't help consumers or the economy.

Much like the government-at-large, the Federal Reserve doesn't provide solutions to our financial problems—it is the problem. My dad not only wrote the foreword to Woods' book, but he has spent his entire political career trying to educate the public about the problems inherent in central banking and the Federal Reserve.

And it's working.

End the Fed?

The Fed is using all its power to drive the monetary base to unprecedented heights, creating trillions in new money out of thin air. From April 2008 to April 2009, the adjusted monetary base shot up from $856 billion to an unbelievable $1.749 trillion. Was there any new wealth created? New production? No, this was the Ben Bernanke printing press at work. If you and I did anything similar, we would be called counterfeiters and be sent away for a lifetime in prison. But, when the Fed does it—complete with a scientific

gloss—it is seen as the perfectly legal and responsible con-
duct of monetary policy.

Ron Paul, *End the Fed*

On election night, there were over a thousand people crowded
into the Bowling Green Convention Center. Jimmy Vaughan,
the famous blues guitarist, volunteered to play for us that
night; and my boys Duncan and Robert put on a guitar performance, playing "TNT" by Australian hard rockers AC/
DC, as my family walked on stage.

My father introduced me via a streaming Internet video,
and the moment he appeared there were wild calls from the
audience. Like so many crowds who had gathered throughout the campaign, the majority of people were there because
of our own campaign. But that night, as always, there was
an undercurrent of folks who you just knew were die-hard
Ron Paul fans. Halfway into my victory speech I could hear
the chants begin, as they almost always did, "End the Fed!
End the Fed!" And while I agree with my father's critique of
the Fed, I hadn't really talked much about it on the campaign
trail.

In 2009, my father introduced legislation to audit the
Federal Reserve, which garnered over 300 supporters in a
Democrat-controlled House. Senator DeMint followed Dad's
lead in the Senate, introducing sister legislation that was
cosponsored by Senator Bernie Sanders. Since the Federal
Reserve was created in 1913, there has been no oversight, and
in addition to its questionable policies, some of which I've outlined in this book, in 2009 it was reported that the Fed could
not account for $9 trillion in its off-balance sheet transactions.

Yes, you read that right—$9 trillion. After the midterm election the Fed announced it was going to inject $600 billion into the economy through yet another round of "quantitative easing," which once again, means simply printing money out of thin air. This is economic madness.

I will be a proponent in the Senate of a real, meaningful and long overdue audit of the Federal Reserve and will introduce my father's legislation from the House in the Senate. For some time I have believed that auditing the Fed is likely the best or most advanced reform we could possibly hope for.

Yet, despite the thousands of young people who flocked to my father's rallies chanting "End the Fed," I haven't felt that the momentum has existed to significantly change, reform or even come close to actually ending or abolishing the Federal Reserve.

What is encouraging, though, is that immediately after the midterm elections, Sen. Bob Corker and Rep. Mike Pence came out publicly for stripping the Fed of some of its power. *The New York Times* reported in November: "Criticism of the Federal Reserve intensified on Tuesday as conservative Republican lawmakers called for limiting the central bank's mandate to keeping inflation low. They said that the Fed should stop trying to pursue the twin goals of balancing inflation and unemployment, as it has been required to do since 1977... The Fed is rare among central banks in having a dual mandate. Under federal law, it has two equal objectives—maintaining price stability and maximizing employment."

Corker and Pence argue, correctly, that the Fed's oft-preferred remedy for economic recessions, what it calls "quantitative easing"—printing new money out of thin air—only devalues the dollar and does not help us in the economic long term. The notion that such irresponsible financial actions help job growth is absurd. That this responsibility concerning employment should fall on the Fed is something the Founders could have never foreseen and would have deplored.

To follow Corker and Pence's lead by altering the part of the Federal Reserve's mandate that calls for full employment and only give it a mandate to protect the dollar—this alone would be an amazing turn of events.

If we can get a real audit, then our next step would be to restrain and or devolve power away from the Fed's so-called "Open Market Committee," which allows them to manipulate and distort day-to-day interest rates. Interest rates are the ubiquitous "signal" that haunts and habituates all transactions. Creating interest rates below the market rate of interest ignites the boom phase. Keeping interest rates below the market rate allows the economy to become overheated and keeps the economy from correcting itself.

After a real audit, my next step will be to call for limits on the Federal Reserve's power to manipulate interest rates. Americans, and much of the world, had to learn the hard way in 2007 and beyond, how the Fed's intervention did more harm than good, giving rise to unintended consequences the government didn't predict and claimed no one else did either.

Austrian economists did predict the financial crisis, knowing that such intervention in the free market inevitably leads to more and even worse problems. In their wisdom, the Founding Fathers—whose Constitution was supposed to restrain our rulers—would have likely made the same prediction.

Jefferson wrote, "My reading of history convinces me that most bad government results from too much government." This has certainly been true of too much government intervention, as well as attempts to administer too many government benefits.

9

★ ★ ★

Social Security Isn't Secure, Government Healthcare Isn't Healthy

I am for doing good to the poor, but I differ in opinion of the means. I think the best way of doing good to the poor, is not making them easy in poverty, but leading or driving them out of it. In my youth I travelled much, and I observed in different countries, that the more public provisions were made for the poor, the less they provided for themselves, and of course became poorer. And, on the contrary, the less was done for them, the more they did for themselves, and became richer.

Benjamin Franklin

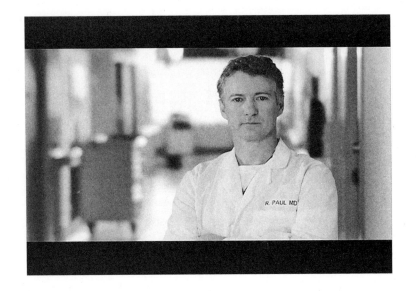

In my speech to the 9/12 Project in Danville, Kentucky, I explained that in medicine we have a term called *homeostasis*, which means a maintaining of balance. When you eat a large meal, your blood glucose rises and insulin rises in response. This increase of insulin then normalizes your blood glucose, bringing it down.

This process is similar to what should have happened during the mortgage crisis. As the economy heats up and homebuilders build more, the price of homes falls, sending a signal to the market to build fewer homes. Also, as more and more homes are built, the competition for money increases and the price of the money—interest—also begins to rise. When interest rates rise they send a signal to the economy, like insulin. The economy then slowly cools until prices and interest rates reach such a low point that building and growth resumes.

Why is this tedious explanation necessary? Because if we don't understand what caused the financial crisis and subsequent recession we are doomed to repeat the policies that created the problem in the first place. It is not an academic exercise to ask, "What caused the Great Depression?" Nor is it irrelevant to ask, "What caused the current Great Recession?" If we let emotions rule, and allow our hearts, not our brains, to take control, we are destined to repeat and make worse the current situation.

As I traveled across Kentucky during the campaign, criss-crossing the state, talking about the Federal Reserve's policies, interest rates, and recessions, the professional pundits said I didn't "get it." They said that politicians aren't supposed to talk that way about economics, and aren't supposed to get into so many details. No, politicians are supposed to kiss babies, speak in sound bites and avoid long answers at all costs, or so I was told.

I was told I didn't "get" Kentucky because I didn't talk about specific projects that I would bring to every county.

I couldn't do it. I still can't. For too long, we have desperately needed a national adult conversation about our entitlement programs, which are rapidly becoming insolvent. Instead the media hounded me for not detailing the pork I would bring home. I responded that I would advocate for Kentucky but only in terms of a balanced budget. It made no sense to me to borrow money from China or print it at the Fed to pay for projects, even in my home state.

The pundits said it couldn't be done. They said no politician could win statewide by telling the truth that we, as a nation, were broke.

Luckily, in the midterm elections, there was a nationwide movement hungry for serious and substantive answers. And thanks to the Tea Party, more Americans than ever seem willing to listen.

An Adult Conversation About Entitlements

From a purely political standpoint, if Republicans think that remaining silent on (Social Security) will protect them from Democratic attacks, they are the stupid party indeed.
Michael D. Tanner, Cato Institute Senior Fellow

When Ronald Reagan tried to reform Social Security, House Speaker Tip O'Neill dubbed it the "third rail of American politics." When George W. Bush tried to reform Social Security, he found the issue too toxic to tackle despite having Republican majorities in Congress. When I began to talk on the campaign trail about the need for serious reform of both Social Security and Medicare, my Democratic opponent did what Democrats often do—dishonestly accused me of wanting to cut or get rid of these programs. On the campaign trail, seniors would approach me wanting to know if what my opponent had said about me cutting Social Security was true. For a lot of these seniors, Social Security was pretty much all they had, and they relied heavily on Medicare. I allayed their fears and promised that I would not touch or alter payments for current retirees, unless they had the means to afford the changes. Most voters feared changes but many admitted that something had to be done, and I don't think we lost many votes because of my willingness to discuss entitlement reform.

Our sound-bite culture leads to such misperceptions, and these personal conversations were indicative of just how difficult it is to discuss entitlement reform. Much like our big and bloated foreign policy, many might recognize that we don't have the money to continue with these massive undertakings indefinitely, yet hardly anyone is willing to address the obvious—much less do something about it.

Entitlements represent the largest part of our budget and debt. There is no "fund" in which the federal government takes money out of your check and sets it aside for Social Security or Medicare. The politicians have already spent it, and continue to spend it. Last year the Pax Americana Institute released a report entitled *Social Security Insolvency Could Occur Earlier Than Predicted*. The report forecast "massive and permanent deficits if Congress fails to reform this dilapidated and outmoded entitlement program." Consider the details of this pressing problem:

> In 1950, there were fifty workers for every one recipient of Social Security, whereas, today, there are three workers for every one beneficiary. By 2040, Social Security, Medicare and Medicaid will consume one-hundred percent of federal expenditures.... The long-term costs associated with the current government run entitlement programs (Social Security, Medicare, and Medicaid) pose a fatal threat to America's economic supremacy. Social Security's exorbitant unfunded liabilities, $27 trillion over the next seventy-five years, will be demonstrably bad for American economic supremacy. In the next seventy-five years, the Social Security Trust Fund will owe $79 million more than it will receive in payroll taxes.

Let me repeat that: Entitlements will consume the entire budget within a few decades. If you add in interest, entitlements plus interest will consume the entire budget in a little over a decade. Is it any wonder that Admiral Mullen, Defense

Secretary Gates and others have said that the biggest threat to our national security is our debt?

The Cato Institute's Michael Tanner and author of *Leviathan on the Right: How Big-Government Conservatism Brought Down the Republican Revolution*, wrote in August at *National Review Online*:

> There is no doubt that Social Security desperately needs reform. Social Security is already running a temporary deficit, and that deficit will turn permanent in just five years. In theory, the Social Security Trust Fund will pay benefits until 2037. That's not much comfort to today's 35-year-olds, who will face a 27 percent cut in benefits unless the program is reformed before they retire. But even that figure is misleading, because the trust fund contains no actual assets. The government bonds it holds are simply IOUs, a measure of how much money the government owes the system. It says nothing about where the government will get the $2.6 trillion to pay off those IOUs.... Even if Congress can find a way to redeem the bonds, the trust-fund surplus will be completely exhausted by 2037. At that point, Social Security will have to rely solely on revenue from the payroll tax—and that won't be sufficient to pay all the promised benefits. Overall, the amount the system has promised beyond what it can actually pay now totals $18.7 trillion.

Tanner adds: "But Republican leaders, battered by the failure of President Bush's reform initiative and years of Democratic demagoguery, show no signs of venturing back into this issue. In fact, the only senior Republican willing to support personal accounts these days appears to be Rep. Paul Ryan, who has included in his 'roadmap' a plan to allow younger workers the option of investing slightly less than half of their Social Security taxes. However, it is telling that Ryan's roadmap has just 13 co-sponsors, none of whom are among the Republican leadership."

It is also worth mentioning that Ryan's plan is something that would be implemented over the span of nearly six decades. We don't have six decades to fix entitlements. And still, as Tanner points out, most Republicans are afraid to go anywhere near this issue.

As I promised the seniors who supported me in Kentucky, we won't do anything to change benefits for those currently receiving Social Security or Medicare. But we do have to admit that we have the baby boomers getting ready to retire; subsequently doubling the amount of people already dependent on an unsustainable system. To put our head in the sand and just say we're going to keep borrowing more money simply will not work. We must reform the program for younger Americans, including adjusting eligibility requirements. To sustain our current system, we may have to raise the retirement age for future generations. The average life expectancy in the 1930s was about 65. Obviously this is no longer the case, and for younger Americans, a relatively increased longevity makes such changes possible. If they're honest about entitlements, willing to have an adult conversation and not demagogue the issue, younger generations will have to accept different rules concerning entitlements.

Decades of wasteful spending by career politicians in Washington has drained the Social Security and Medicare trust funds. Reported *The Christian Science Monitor*'s Patrick Chisolm in 2005:

The Social Security contributions that do not get spent on current retirees are commingled with general funds, going toward government salaries, departmental budgets, pork-barrel projects, foreign aid, and the many other things that the government spends money on. Not a penny of it is ever saved for workers' retirement. In the private sector, that would be grounds for certain conviction. To top it off, government officials have the effrontery to claim that there's a Social Security "trust fund." But this merely refers to how much the US Treasury—i.e. the US taxpayer—owes the Social Security Administration. If United Airlines executives told their employees that the $9.8 billion in underfunded pension liabilities is a "trust fund," they'd be sued for fraud.

The combination of the resulting massive debt, fewer active workers, and more retirees is pushing Social Security and Medicare to the brink of bankruptcy. In fact, for the first time in the program's history, this year Social Security will pay out more in benefits than is paid in by workers. Part of Medicare reached that same troubling milestone several years ago.

Unlike most politicians, I will not pander. I will speak the truth about entitlements. I am not afraid to start a bipartisan discussion regarding practical and realistic changes to Social Security and Medicare that must take place if we expect these programs to continue for our children and grandchildren. Any changes discussed would only apply to younger Americans who have time to plan for the future. Americans fifty-five and under might be a good place to start. It's also hard to imagine saving Social Security without eventually raising the age for collecting benefits to seventy. We might even have to start using "means testing," in which we would determine to what degree some actually need benefits. The alternative is a bankrupt entitlement system that will take care of no one, not the least of which are those currently dependent upon these soon-to-be-insolvent programs.

The Obamacare Disaster

> *If you think health care is expensive now, wait until you see what it costs when it's free.*
> P. J. O'Rourke

When the Democrats pushed through Obamacare it wasn't unlike federal stimulus, TARP or the PATRIOT act legislation before it—government had to act immediately we were told and, in their haste, politicians would claim that the urgency of the situation was more important than any of the many details in the bill, however major or minor. Those details, however, have been far more major than most Americans could have ever fathomed.

The *American Thinker*'s Janice Shaw Crouse explains some of the details:

> ObamaCare contains $670 billion in tax increases. For the middle class, there are at least 14 different tax increases signed into law that target taxpayers making less than $250,000 per year. In Massachusetts, a state that enacted health care reforms similar to the national plan, more than a half-dozen lawsuits were filed to stop double-digit premium increases. The *Boston Globe*

warned that ObamaCare could result in similar lawsuits at the federal level.

Crouse adds: "(Government) officials are owning up to what most Americans already knew. Obamacare means higher costs and lower quality; Obamacare means rationing and higher taxes—including a Value Added Tax (VAT). It means mandating and penalties. President Obama and his liberal colleagues on the Hill jettisoned the world's best health-care system for the dubious honor of having achieved 'health care reform.'"

On the campaign trail I would often tell voters that Obamacare created not a single new doctor—but over 4,000 new IRS agents. I was wrong. According to *The Washington Examiner* 16,500 new IRS workers would have to be hired to enforce Obamacare. Yes, I said "enforce." Reported *USA Today* after the legislation's passage:

Internal Revenue Service agents already try to catch tax cheats and moonshiners. Under the proposed health care legislation, they would get another assignment: checking to see whether Americans have health insurance. The legislation would require most Americans to have health insurance and to prove it on their federal tax returns. Those who don't would pay a penalty to the IRS. That's one of several key duties the IRS would assume under the bills that have been approved by the House of Representatives and Senate and will be merged by negotiators from both chambers.

There are so many hidden aspects to Obamacare that they are hard to wrap one's head around and, last year, Americans for Tax Reform released a breakdown of the bill, called "By the Numbers." Some of the items found were the following:

- The number of new tax increases in the healthcare bill: 19
- The number of tax increases that unquestionably violate President Obama's "firm pledge" not to raise "any form" of taxes on families making less than $250,000: 7
- The tax increase over the first decade if the healthcare bill becomes law: $497 billion
- The top federal tax rate on wages and self-employment earnings under this bill: 43.4%
- The top federal tax rate on early distributions from HSAs [health savings accounts] under this bill: 59.6%
- The most parents of special-needs kids can save tax-free for tuition in FSAs [flexible spending accounts] (currently, the amount is unlimited): $2,500

In a story by *Kiplinger's* last year entitled "Health Care Reform: 13 Tax Changes on the Way," it was reported that Obamacare included: "A limit on the amount that employees can contribute to health care flexible spending accounts to $2,500 a year...[which] was previously left to the employer's discretion, with many firms choosing a limit of $4,000 to $5,000 or so...A new tax on individuals who don't obtain adequate health coverage by 2014—this is often referred to as the individual mandate...A nondeductible fee charged to businesses with 50 or more employees if the firms fail to offer adequate coverage..."

The burden on businesses and individuals described above is only the tip of the iceberg when it comes to the many troublesome details of Obamacare. Also included is a 10 percent tax on tanning salons. There is also a hidden tax on Medicare for those who earn over a certain amount. And to be sure, this is not the only hidden tax, on Medicare or otherwise.

Ironically enough, during the election, my Democratic opponent accused me of wanting to cut Medicare benefits for current recipients. Interestingly enough, the Democrats' government-run healthcare law does exactly that. Reports the Heritage Foundation's Conn Carroll:

> Over one in five Medicare patients is enrolled in the Medicare Advantage plans that President Obama wants to completely cut. The benefits that over 10.5 million seniors would probably lose as a result of President Obama's $200 billion in Medicare Advantage cuts include: prescription drug coverage, preventive-care services, coordinated care for chronic conditions, routine physical examinations, additional hospitalization, skilled nursing facility stays, routine eye and hearing examinations (and) glasses and hearing aids.

When Thomas Jefferson wrote that a "government big enough to give you everything you want is big enough to take away everything you have," he could have easily been referencing Obamacare.

Speaking with a group of business owners in Lexington, Kentucky, during the election, none of them seem pleased that Obamacare would require filing 1099 forms on every business transaction exceeding $600. We discussed the fact that deductibles had already gone up under Obamacare. We discussed the fact that Obama admired the British healthcare system, which is practically bankrupt. We also agreed that government-run healthcare, particularly as monstrous and as micromanagerial as the legislation the Democrats passed, would inevitably lead to rationing.

Everyone attacked Sarah Palin and Glenn Beck for their talk of "death panels" during the debate over healthcare, but there was some truth in their statements. I went on national television to say that they may not unplug Grandma, they just won't plug her in to begin with. In fact, we already have "death panels" that deny certain chemotherapies. In one of the most egregious examples, a woman in Oregon received a letter from the government insurance agency that stated her chemotherapy was not covered under their program but "physician aid-in-dying" was offered to her—also known as assisted suicide.

Wrote the *Detroit Free Press*'s Michael F. Cannon during the debate over Obamacare:

> The intelligentsia have been quick to dismiss former Alaska governor Sarah Palin's claim that, under President Obama's health plan, "my parents or my baby with Down Syndrome will have to stand in front of Obama's 'death panel' so his bureaucrats can decide...whether they are worthy of health care." No one ever accused Palin of being a health policy expert, and many found her hyperbolic term "death panel" off-putting. But that should not distract voters from this reality: President Obama has proposed a new body that would enhance Medicare's ability to deny care to the elderly and disabled based on government bureaucrats' arbitrary valuations of those patients' lives. It is right there in the legislation now before Congress, and it is called the Independent Medicare Advisory Council.

Cannon added: "Whatever one thinks of Sarah Palin should not distract from this truth: President Obama proposes to let government bureaucrats decide who gets medical care and who does not."

The *American Spectator*'s Peter Ferrara, author of the "The Obamacare Disaster: An Appraisal of the Patient Protection and Affordable Care Act" offered one of the more ominous outlooks on the implications of Obamacare:

> The bottom line is that you will lose your health care under this legislation, if not your job, your country as they bankrupt America, and maybe ultimately your life or the life of a loved one. All that to make dreamy, emotionalized, liberals happy, even though many of them are not happy because the socialism in the bill is not overt enough. Moreover, the promises made to the American people to pass the bill are shown in the study to be thoroughly false. This pattern of calculated deception, however, did not fool the American people, only members of Congress, many of whom will now pay with their jobs as a result.

My father made perhaps the most important point about Obamacare, a point that will continue to affect every aspect of our runaway government: "I don't think it will improve medical care in this country. I think it's very, very costly and we don't have any money. And they don't have any way of paying for it."

The Democrats claimed that Obamacare would cost $1.2 trillion but not add anything to the debt. I told audiences that I didn't believe it and I didn't meet anyone in Kentucky who did. It is incomprehensible to me that when Social Security and

Medicare are short of money and increasingly unable to fund the retiring baby boomers, we would add a new entitlement program. We can't fund the existing entitlement programs and the Democrats blithely added the largest entitlement program in recent times.

My father also made the point that Obamacare, or the very concept of having a "right" to healthcare, undermines not only the free market but some of the most basic precepts of American life and liberty:

> Political philosopher Richard Weaver famously and correctly stated that ideas have consequences. Take for example ideas about rights versus goods. Natural law states that people have rights to life, liberty and the pursuit of happiness. A good is something you work for and earn. It might be a need, like food, but more "goods" seem to be becoming "rights" in our culture, and this has troubling consequences. It might seem harmless enough to decide that people have a right to things like education, employment, housing or healthcare. But if we look a little further into the consequences, we can see that the workings of the community and economy are thrown wildly off balance when people accept those ideas.

An Adult Conversation About Healthcare Reform

Because of all of the problems created by Obamacare, the misshapen legislation is just the beginning, not the end, of the battle to reform health care policy in America.

Obamacare is so fundamentally wrong-headed that it takes us in the opposite direction of the essential reforms that are needed. Perhaps such a disastrously wrong step was necessary to draw the public's attention to the true patient power reforms that would liberate health care in America.

Peter Ferrara, "The Obamacare Disaster"
American Spectator, August 18, 2010

Republicans failed to acknowledge that the distribution of healthcare in the United States had some imperfections, namely cost and access. We were often good at regaling how America was the envy of the world in healthcare, or about how foreign dignitaries often come to the United States for treatment, but we were not forthright in admitting the deficiencies of our system.

As a physician, the number one complaint I hear is about cost, not access. Insurance premiums have been climbing faster than inflation and are a concern to both individuals and employers who provide insurance. The question is: do we think more government involvement in healthcare is the answer? Or should it be more capitalism and greater competition?

Everywhere you look in our economy, where capitalism thrives, prices decline and productivity increases. We should inject more capitalism into healthcare, not less. One example of where free-market solutions have worked is Lasik eye surgery. While general healthcare costs continue to rise, the cost for Lasik eye surgery has decreased by over half since the procedure's inception. The reason is, since this type of eye surgery is not covered by most insurance plans, doctors have had to compete for patients' business. This demonstrates how, when prices aren't skewed by insurance mandates and government interference, health-related procedures go down in cost as time goes on, just like all other goods.

About half of all healthcare is now distributed or administered by the government, either through Medicare for senior citizens or Medicaid for the indigent. The overall costs of these programs rise dramatically each year for one simple reason—the costs are not borne by the user. These costs would be better controlled if the patients bore more of the costs of the service. This answer, though, is a bitter pill to swallow for those who now enjoy being subsidized by the taxpayer.

Bearing more of the cost would mean higher copays, higher deductibles and higher premiums. The question is: how high and who pays? Any increase in copayments for Medicaid will have to be modest, but we don't want to enlarge Medicaid to include even more recipients. Estimates are that Obamacare will add 16 million new people to Medicaid. The Democrats have proposed adding folks to the "indigent" Medicaid rolls that earn up to $88,000 annually—hardly a salary considered at or below the poverty level.

For private insurance, the best way to lower premiums is to encourage competition across state lines and encourage high-deductible health savings accounts (HSAs). One of the best legislative changes in recent years was to allow HSAs to roll over from year to year. In the past, HSAs expired at the end of the year, and it was a use-it-or-lose-it plan that didn't allow for ongoing expenses. HSAs with high deductibles allow lower premiums, with the ability to save money and build wealth over time to cover expenses such as orthodontia. HSAs also create a marketplace that drives down healthcare costs by empowering patients to control their healthcare decisions. By contrast, Obamacare limits the use of HSAs by limiting what types of healthcare expenses can be expended from your HSA.

Obamacare primarily was directed at increasing access but really doesn't do anything to lower the actual expense of health services. In fact, Obamacare's effect on expense will likely be to raise the cost of healthcare, as it adds in new mandates such as insuring adult children to age twenty-six and eliminating the ability to charge more for sicker individuals. At first blush it seems very noble to prevent insurance companies from charging sick people more for their insurance—but you must also realize what happens when you prevent them from charging healthy people less.

When you legislate away the use of pre-existing conditions, you pervert market incentives. Normally, healthy people have an incentive to buy insurance before they become ill because it is too expensive to buy after one becomes ill. Under Obamacare, the opposite incentive exists. If I can buy it for the same price after I become ill, why not wait until I have chest pain and am rolling into the ER to buy my insurance? I might save ten years of insurance premiums by not buying health insurance until I'm sick or injured. Insurance works because we have large pools of healthy people buying insurance. Insurance becomes top-heavy with sick people if you give an incentive for healthy people to opt out.

How can we fix some of the inequities that occur when people contract significant illnesses such as heart disease, cancer or rheumatologic disease, which become designated as pre-existing conditions? One way would be to tweak the tax code to encourage the sale of multiyear health insurance policies. Currently, term life insurance is sold in multiyear policies, so if you have a heart attack and survive, your term life insurance doesn't increase in price. Why? Because term life insurance is sold in multiyear policies. But your health insurance, because it's a one-year policy, can skyrocket or worse yet—the insurance company could drop you. We could avoid this bad situation if we could purchase multiyear health insurance policies.

When the Democrats began to push for a takeover of healthcare by the federal government, they would always point to the 45 million Americans without health insurance. But no one mentioned that every one of the 45 million actually had 100 percent access to emergency care. Since hospitals became commonplace, even before government healthcare, it has always been a policy to turn no one away from emergency care.

The Democrats also didn't really tell you who these uninsured folks were. Approximately, one-third of them are eligible for Medicaid but haven't bothered to sign up for it because they consider the process a hassle. These folks simply head down to the local emergency room whenever they're sick. The Democrats forgot to note that this segment of the uninsured already has a place to go: Medicaid. Another third of the uninsured make more than $50,000 per year and don't buy insurance because of the cost. The trick to helping this segment become insured is to address the cost of insurance and give them information about low-cost HSAs. Some estimate that about 40 percent of the uninsured are without insurance for less than a year, as they make the transition from school to work, or from their first job to a job with insurance.

Another third of the uninsured are said to be illegal immigrants. I don't think we should drive the healthcare debate with how we give free insurance to people who broke the law to be in this country to begin with. Media pundits claim that Obamacare won't give taxpayer money to illegal aliens, but the truth is much murkier. During the debates over Obamacare, Republicans asked that amendments be added that included verification of citizenship or legal status for patients before they received taxpayer dollars. The Democrats rejected these amendments. So while the bill says no illegal immigrants will receive coverage, the truth is that *no one* is authorized, required or obligated to ask if patients are in the country legally. This is the charade our leaders go through. And then they wonder why so many Americans are annoyed with Washington politicians.

The bottom line is that there is always a choice we can make—a fork in the road—each time we discuss how to reform healthcare. Do we choose a government solution or a market solution? The government solution does nothing to lower healthcare costs, forces people to purchase insurance, features countless new hidden taxes and regulations, disrupts current plans or makes it attractive for employers to discontinue them, takes over one-sixth of the economy and drastically changes the entire culture of medical services. Plus, we can't afford it.

I want to seek out, explain, and extol the market solution. Why? Because the market works—and is the best practical solution to nearly every problem we face.

But perhaps even more important, the "marketplace" is just another name for a free society; a society based on voluntary transactions, where the citizens are at liberty to make their own decisions instead of having government mandates foisted upon them.

This is precisely the type of society our Founders envisioned.

10

★ ★ ★

We Don't Have a Revenue Problem, We Have a Spending Problem

"We just can't afford it!" Not long ago, every American child heard that, at one time or another, in the home in which he or she was raised. "We just can't afford it!" It may have been a new car, or two weeks at the beach, or the new flat-panel TV screen. Every family knew there were times you had to do without...How many times in the last decade have the political leaders of either party stood up and declared, "No, we cannot afford this..." Does either party have any plan to cut federal spending from today's near 28 percent of GDP to the more traditional 21 percent? George W. Bush didn't even try, and Obama is making that Great Society Republican president look like Ron Paul.

Pat Buchanan, "The Fatal Flaw of Democracies," August 24, 2009

* * *

I spoke with the president one day in mid-November. On the phone from Air Force One, he congratulated me on my victory and apologized for not calling me earlier, as he had been in India. I told him that I wanted him to know that the Tea Party wanted a polite and civil discourse, and that I would always work to make the discussion a productive one. The president responded that we can agree to disagree without being disagreeable. I told him that I was a Republican who wished to end our two wars in a safe and expeditious fashion and that we might find common ground there. He responded that he was a Democrat who was concerned about the debt and we agreed that we might find areas of common ground.

On the debt, especially—I pray he's right.

When I appeared on CBS's *Face the Nation* after the election, host Bob Schieffer asked me, "Polls show overwhelmingly that voters want the two sides to find compromise. Did you come to Washington to compromise?" I responded, "I think there is room for compromise. I think that overwhelmingly the polls also show that people are concerned about the debt, and you have reasonable people saying that one of our biggest threats to our national security is the debt."

This is not only true, but it's important that Americans

consider both the magnitude and imminent nature of this threat. The *Washington Monthly*'s Gregg Easterbrook wrote in 2008:

> It took the United States 209 years, from 1789 to 1998, to compile the first $5 trillion in national debt. It has taken just ten years to compile the second $5 trillion. The national debt was $5.7 trillion when George W. Bush took office; currently it is set to rise to $11.3 trillion. Want another shocker number? Just a generation ago, in 1980, the national debt ceiling was $2.3 trillion, stated in today's dollars; in a single generation, the debt has quintupled....
>
> Although much of the debt liability was incurred when Republicans controlled all three branches of government, undisciplined, irresponsible borrowing in Washington has become the norm for both parties.

Indeed it has. When Bush left office, a $12 trillion debt required Congress to raise the debt ceiling to $13 trillion and now, under Obama, a $13.7 trillion debt required Congress to raise the ceiling to $14 trillion—at least for the moment. Most observers agree that the debt ceiling will "need" to be raised again. If it took two centuries to accumulate $5 trillion in debt, and only the last decade to more than double that amount—under both Republican and Democratic administrations—what will the next few years or a decade hold if government continues on the same trajectory?

In my interview with Schieffer, I repeated my concern that Republicans always want to cut domestic spending but never the military, while Democrats want to cut the military but never domestic spending, and that ignoring either makes significant debt reduction impossible. Inspired, or perhaps in some cases prodded, by the Tea Party, many Republicans now appear serious about cutting domestic spending and an increasing number are willing to look at military spending. This is encouraging. To their credit, President Obama and Defense Secretary Gates seem willing to make necessary cuts in military spending or, as CNN quoted Defense Secretary Gates last spring, "The Pentagon must hold down its spending and make choices that will anger 'powerful people' in an era of economic strain."

What is not encouraging is that too many in both parties still show too much hesitance in changing business-as-usual in Washington, every aspect of which must be substantively reformed or, in many cases, rejected. We must look at everything across the board when cutting government because, quite literally, *everything* must be looked at.

The national debt is the greatest crisis we face. If in the past politicians have acted in great haste to expand government every time there's been other supposed crises—why can't politicians from both parties now become just as pro-active in cutting government to fix this crisis?

Why We Must Balance the Budget

The state is the great fiction by which everyone seeks to live at the expense of everyone else.
Frédéric Bastiat

Bastiat was an early nineteenth-century theorist and economist, and he was absolutely right about the state being a great fiction. The question is: how long can that great fiction continue? For too long Washington has told us that we can live at the expense of future generations—that we merely "owe it to ourselves." But if the financial crisis taught us anything, it is that our decisions have long-term implications and we cannot continue to ignore economic reality.

Balancing the budget is no longer an academic question but an economic imperative. We are drowning in a sea of debt and the repercussions will come sooner rather than later. I do not believe the debt will simply burden future generations. I believe we will begin to pay for it in the next few years through significant inflation. If we continue along our current course we may see 1979-style inflation, 15 to 20 percent or more. Imagine the turmoil when a fourth of one's savings is lost in a year, or a fourth of one's income is lost. Imagine what happens to citizens on fixed incomes.

For every dollar the government spends, it must tax a dollar from the real economy. This means that it is a mathematical fact that we must choose between having government spending and economic growth—we can't have both. Just as it is irresponsible for an individual to spend more than he takes in, it is just as irresponsible for the federal government to do the same. Balancing the budget is important precisely because it forces Washington and the current administration to contend with fiscal reality.

But the federal government does not like to deal with reality. It likes to operate in a fantasyland where money grows on trees and deficits don't matter. But deficits do matter because at some point we have to pay the piper.

We pay for government in three ways: direct taxation, borrowing, and printing money.

The first is the most visible. When the government taxes, it takes money from entrepreneurs, capitalists and businessmen and gives it to government contractors, politicians, and bureaucrats. The more money that ends up in the hands of politicians, the less money there is in the hands of people who actually contribute to society. It's that simple.

The second way the government finances itself is through borrowing. While many Americans buy government bonds, much of our debt is held by foreign governments. According to the Treasury Department, countries like China, Japan and others are holding about $4 trillion in US debt. This creates a dangerous situation where our government makes policy based on what's in the best interest of foreign governments and not our own. While free trade is essential to global and American prosperity, government manipulation of currencies is not.

But the final, most pernicious way government tries to evade economic reality is, as I've discussed, through the printing press. The Federal Reserve, which controls our nation's money supply, essentially has the power to create new dollars and credit out of thin air. Basic economic principle states that the greater the quantity of any good (including money itself) the less valuable that good is. The more money the Fed creates, the less each dollar in your pocket can buy. So while you aren't taxed directly, your money can buy less and therefore your real income goes down.

Since 1913 we've lost 96 percent of the value of the dollar. I often joked to audiences on the campaign trail that once upon a time the dollar was backed by gold, then after 1971 the dollar was backed by treasury bills, but since 2007 the dollar has been backed by used car loans, derivatives, and various other "toxic" assets that the Fed bought and still largely refuses to acknowledge. The Republicans have lost a lot of credibility because they've campaigned on balanced budgets, but once they get to Washington they spend like Democrats. This is why many Republicans have been losing elections, particularly during GOP primaries. While I was campaigning around the country for my father in 2008, the real story was not who won the Republican primaries, but how few people showed up to vote. People are fed up with politicians who behave irresponsibly and renege on their campaign promises. Instead of pledging to balance the budget in ten or fifteen years, Republicans need to cut spending now. The longer we wait and the more interest accrues on the national debt, the harder it will be to make the cuts down the line.

Thirty-two states require that their legislatures and governors pass balanced budgets. Congress, too, has at various times passed a balanced budget amendment. The Senate passed one in 1982 and the House in 1995. Thirty-two state legislatures passed a balanced budget amendment to the Constitution, two states short of what would be required to call for a Constitutional Convention—and not quite enough to force government to stop the deficits. Still, we are close, and in the current political environment passing such legislation at the federal level is even more possible than ever.

Republicans have, on occasion, been good at cutting taxes, but have never even attempted to cut spending. We must cut across the board. And we must, finally, balance the budget.

Cutting Spending

I place economy among the first and most important vir-
tues, and public debt as the greatest of dangers to be feared.
To preserve our independence, we must not let our rulers
load us with perpetual debt.

Thomas Jefferson

Whenever suggestions are brought up about balancing budgets or cutting spending, politicians try to scare us, behaving
as if the world will come to an end the moment we begin to
reduce government. But consider this: if we simply used the
2002 budget for 2009, we would not be running a deficit.
We would still be spending $2.2 trillion dollars and taking in
roughly the same. Certainly, civilization would not crumble if
the federal government returned to the crude, bare-bones size
it was in 2002.

Yet, government continues to grow at breakneck speed. In
June, *Heritage Foundation* budget analyst Brian Riedl reported:

The 2010 edition of "Federal Spending by the Numbers" shows spending and deficits continuing to grow
at a pace not seen since World War II. Washington will
spend $30,543 per household in 2010—$5,000 per
household more than just two years ago. While some of
this spending is a temporary result of the recession, President Obama's latest budget would replace this temporary
spending with permanent new programs. Consequently,
by 2020—a time of assumed peace and prosperity—
Washington would still spend nearly $36,000 per

household, compared to $25,000 per household before this recession (adjusted for inflation)....

Since 2000, spending has grown across the board. Entitlement spending has reached a record 14 percent of GDP. Discretionary spending has expanded 79 percent faster than inflation as a result of large defense and domestic spending hikes. Other spending categories that have grown rapidly since 2000 include: anti-poverty programs (89 percent faster than inflation), K–12 education (219 percent), veterans spending (107 percent), and Medicare (81 percent). And despite all the pressing national priorities, lawmakers approved over 9,000 earmarks last year at a cost of $16.5 billion. Simply put, all parts of government are growing.

Those receiving Social Security, Medicare, veteran's benefits and other benefits must be taken care of, but these numbers are indicative of just how deep the growth problem is. And as Riedl demonstrates, government growth is out of control and continues to accelerate at an unsustainable rate. As all parts of government grow, all parts must also be looked at. After his first report referenced above, Riedl compiled another report in October entitled "How to Cut $343 Billion from the Federal Budget," in which he discussed "Spending cuts for the new Congress to consider when it takes up the federal budget for FY 2012." Many of the cuts fall into six areas:

- Empowering state and local governments. Congress should focus the federal government on performing a few duties well and allow the state and local governments, which are closer to the people, to creatively address local needs in areas such as transportation, justice, job training, and economic development.

- Consolidating duplicative programs. Past Congresses have repeatedly piled duplicative programs on top of pre-existing programs, increasing administrative costs and creating a bureaucratic maze that confuses people seeking assistance.
- Privatization. Many current government functions could be performed more efficiently by the private sector.
- Targeting programs more precisely. Corporate welfare programs benefit those who do not need assistance in the American free enterprise system. Other programs often fail to enforce their own eligibility requirements.
- Eliminating outdated and ineffective programs. Congress often allows the federal government to run the same programs for decades, despite many studies showing their ineffectiveness.
- Eliminating waste, fraud, and abuse. Taxpayers will never trust the federal government to reform major entitlements if they believe that the savings will go toward "bridges to nowhere," vacant government buildings, and Grateful Dead archives."

Riedl concluded: "Almost all of the proposed cuts in federal spending will provoke strong objections from constituencies that benefit from having Members of Congress give them taxpayer money taken from someone else. Yet the difficulties caused by each of these cuts should be measured against the status quo option of doubling the national debt over the next decade, risking an economic crisis, and drowning future generations in taxes."

As I said when I debated in front of the farm bureau, "I can't argue to continue programs that pay dead farmers not to farm. I can't argue to continue to borrow money from China to pay non-farmers not to farm." One of the most egregious farm subsidy scandals is a 95-acre subdivision in Austin County, Texas, divided into quarter acre lots with homes, but no farms. The homeowners are still receiving cash payment from the federal government to not grow crops.

If you talk to politicians from both parties, they will give many excuses as to why certain accelerated spending is warranted, often carving out particular niches to please constituents back home or campaign contributors. The process, most often referred to as "earmarking" or "earmarks," is not a significant part of the budget—but like every other part of the budget—each part now becomes significant in the overall battle to bring down the debt.

Why Earmarks Must End

Shortly before the election, a Kentucky university president asked to have lunch with me. You tend to know your chances of winning are going up when those who receive federal largesse want to meet you and the election is still two weeks away.

We had a pleasant lunch, and afterward he handed me a list of earmarks that other Kentucky politicians had brought home to his university. Before I could reply he said, "I know you've taken a position on earmarks and I respect that, but the debt is a problem, and I'm an American first." He was telling me that he agreed with me that our debt problem was paramount above all others. I fully inhaled his statement and savored it:

"I'm an American first." Sitting before me was a very successful university president whose primary job was to advocate for
his university—and here he was acknowledging that America
faces such a debt crisis, that maybe it was time to elect someone who is not just a rubber stamp for earmarks for his state.

I walked away proud that I might be part of a movement
that could put America first, and ahead of petty, provincial
pork barrel spending. Maybe America was waking up. Maybe
the dire nature of our crisis would awaken the entire nation,
long addicted to federal largesse, to finally say, "Enough
is enough—we cannot continue to spend money we do not
have."

And things are changing. During the campaign I took a
pledge not to place earmarks on bills. Without question the
Tea Party is annoyed and offended by earmarks, particularly
earmarks tacked on to unrelated bills that specify millions of
dollars to random items like "Tom Smith's Museum" in a small
town somewhere. Often such Tom Smiths are political donors,
or perhaps his granddaughter is, and the earmark is a special
homage—at the taxpayer's expense—to the Smith family.

Now some would argue, including my dad, that earmarking
is simply Congress utilizing their Constitutional role to des-
ignate where the money is spent. Wrote my father in his book
The Revolution: A Manifesto:

> Instead of talking about how we might restore fiscal san-
> ity to the federal budget, the political establishment tries
> to distract us with phony issues like the debate over "ear-
> marks," legislative provisions that direct federal money
> to local projects. One need not look very hard to finds
> examples of abuses in earmarks. But even if all earmarks

were eliminated we would not necessarily save a single penny in the federal budget. Earmarks are funded from spending levels that have been determined before a single earmark is agreed to, so spending levels remain the same with or without earmarks.

I usually agree with my dad; however, it is now beyond dispute that the practice of earmarking has exploded from a few hundred per bill to thousands per bill. In their book *Red State Uprising*, authors Erick Erickson and Lewis K. Uhler note that in 1987 Reagan was denouncing 152 earmarks as far too many—yet in 2003 there were 6,371 earmarks in just one of Bush's transportation bills. Such is the nature of our federal government.

Earmark supporters say the issue is between Congress designating the spending and the president making that designation. In reality, it is more complicated than that. Some of the funds, if not earmarked, are, or can be, sent back to the states and the state legislatures decide how that money is spent.

Earmark supporters also argue that the amount of money earmarked is less than 1 percent of the budget. This may be true, but earmarks are used as an enticement to get representatives to vote for much larger appropriation bills, and the actual dollar amount of the earmarks underestimates the total dollars that are lured out of the treasury by this practice. Sen. Tom Coburn addressed the accusation that stopping earmarking wouldn't save money at *National Review Online*:

This argument has serious logical inconsistencies. The fact is earmarks do spend real money. If they didn't spend money, why defend them? Stopping an activity that spends money does result in less spending. It's that simple. For instance, Congress spent $16.1 billion on pork in Fiscal Year 2010. If Congress does not do earmarks in 2011, we could save $16.1 billion. In no way is Congress locked into shifting that $16.1 billion to other programs unless it wants to.... It's true that earmarks themselves represent a tiny portion of the budget, but a small rudder can help steer a big ship, which is why I've long described earmarks as the gateway drug to spending addiction in Washington. No one can deny that earmarks like the Cornhusker Kickback have been used to push through extremely costly and onerous bills. Plus, senators know that as the number of earmarks has exploded so has overall spending. In the past decade, the size of government has doubled while Congress approved more than 90,000 earmarks.... Eliminating earmarks will not balance the budget overnight, but it is an important step toward getting spending under control.

When Democrats announced that they were banning earmarks last year, many Republicans applauded them—that is, until the details came out. Senator Jim DeMint called out the Democrats' deception:

It was good news to hear that House Democrats had adopted a ban on earmarks to for-profit companies. The bad news is their version of a ban wouldn't apply to 90 percent of all earmarks. Instead of adopting an all-out ban on earmarks, House Democrats have decided to ban earmarks for for-profit entities, while continuing to green light funding for the next Bridge to Nowhere, ACORN, or to clear the way for the Napa Valley Wine train. House Appropriations Chairman Rep. David Obey told reporters Wednesday that the ban would have stripped 1,000 earmarks from the last budget. What he didn't say is that President Obama signed 11,320 earmarks, worth nearly $32 billion, into law last year....

Citizens Against Government Waste found that Mr. Obey nabbed 64 earmarks worth more than $115 million in 2009. Among them was $335,000 to relocate endangered mussels, $125,000 for a scenic trail and $5 million for lighthouse reconstruction. None of those earmarks would be touched by his ban. Neither would the $1,750,000 House Speaker Nancy Pelosi, California Democrat, secured for the Presidio Heritage Center or the $500,000 earmarked by House Majority Leader Rep. Steny Hoyer, Maryland Democrat, for oyster research....

The truth is that Democrats want the public to believe they're committed to ending the culture of corruption without actually doing it.

Ultimately, ending earmarks is really about ending a practice that often tacks on unrelated spending items to otherwise popular bills, without deliberation in committee, and often without transparency—tacked on in the dead of night by anonymous clerks. How much other legislation (the PATRIOT Act, TARP, bailouts) has been passed this way?

To reduce our debt and control spending, every aspect of government must be looked at—and earmarks must end.

Taxed and Spent Enough Already

> *To compel a man to subsidize with his taxes the propaga-*
> *tion of ideas which he disbelieves and abhors is sinful and*
> *tyrannical.*
>
>   Thomas Jefferson

During the final three months of the campaign, various high-ranking Republicans offered advice about some of my policy positions, recommending that I might want to think long and hard about trotting out certain new ideas that I would then have to defend. I was reminded that when Senator Bunning came out for a national sales tax proposal, he spent weeks defending it. I responded that I wasn't planning any groundbreaking new proposals in the final months of the campaign.

Sometimes things don't work out the way you intend. In the final months of the campaign, a former aide released a statement claiming I supported Representative John Linder's "FAIR Tax" reform, or a national sales tax.

Predictably, my opponent went for the jugular. He ran TV attack ads saying I would add a 23 percent sales tax to everything under the sun. He also neglected to inform voters that the plan would also completely eliminate the income tax and the Internal Revenue Service. Yet, my stating that I was for a national sales tax wasn't exactly true or necessarily false. Doesn't this sound like a politician's answer?

I had mentioned at various times that I was not opposed to the idea of repealing the Sixteenth Amendment, which would eliminate the income tax and replace it with a sales tax that would also feature a generous exemption for the working class and poor. I had also at various times mentioned that I was not opposed to the idea of a flat income tax, also with a generous exemption for the working class and poor.

Yet to me it was most important that we continued to talk about the debt and not tax reform. If the Tea Party can be characterized in a single sentence it is this: We are concerned about the massive level of the debt and worried about passing it on to younger generations. If you go beyond the debt, you will find that the Tea Party indeed feels that it is "Taxed Enough Already," but you won't hear as much about tax reform as you will the bold declaration: "We must cut spending."

I think most Tea Partiers would even accept their current level of taxation if government would seriously begin to cut spending. No issue is more important than spending, and the Tea Party knows it.

Yet most of us certainly want tax reform and I stated repeatedly on the campaign trail that I would support any tax reform that lowered the overall burden and complexity of taxes. The tax code is 16,000 pages long and costs over $239 billion to comply with. The only governmental stimulus package that ever worked was lowering and simplifying taxes.

Our politicians, though, have boxed us in by running up the debt to such extraordinary levels that it makes it hard to entertain tax cuts without first addressing spending. At this critical juncture in our history and in American politics, we simply cannot afford to get distracted from the primary issue of reducing the debt.

Our children can't afford it either.

The Tea Party Corrective

Ron Paul was Right.
Andrew Sullivan, *The Atlantic*

In January 2008, during the Republican presidential campaign, the National Taxpayers Union released a report declaring that my dad was the only remaining presidential candidate who actually would cut spending, based on his proposals. Touting this, my father's campaign issued the following press release: "According to the report, Congressman Paul's proposals would cut government spending by over $150 billion, a conservative estimate of the spending reductions Dr. Paul has proposed. The report concludes that the other remaining Republican candidates, Mitt Romney, John McCain and Mike Huckabee, have proposed spending increases of $19.5 billion, $6.9 billion and $54 billion respectively."

I mention this not to embarrass any fellow Republicans but to point out just how much the political environment has changed. When my father was running for president in 2008, much of the party dismissed him for his willingness to question Pentagon spending and policy, while his opponents basically competed to show who was more in favor of the same Pentagon spending and policies. Today, most Tea Partiers are not only willing to address military spending, but would likely consider $150 billion a rather measly government cut. In 2008, much of the Republican Party considered my dad's spendthrift conservatism too "extreme"—today, the Tea Party would likely think Dad's spending cut proposals at that time weren't extreme enough.

The extreme growth of government in the last decade was bound to create some sort of backlash, and the Tea Party now wields political force that few "experts" could have predicted and many politicians now fear. If, today, the entire Republican Party goes out of its way to sound more like my dad, it is the Tea Party that has created this new environment. Today's Tea Party politics demands serious reform. Yesterday's politics, Republican Party and phony conservatism, simply will not do.

Above all, the Tea Party gives Americans new voice and with it, a new hope: That we might finally be able to put this country back on the right track again.

11

★ ★ ★

Tea Party Revolution

I'm just talking about common sense people who don't think balancing a checkbook is a radical idea. That's what we're looking for now. Because the people in Washington have clearly gotten out of control, in both parties. When you have $13 trillion in debt, you've got a big problem....And Republicans didn't do what we said we were going to do. We spent too much. We borrowed too much. And frankly, if we get the majority again...and we don't do what we say, I think the Republican Party's dead.

Senator Jim DeMint

Growing up, I met many interesting people as the son of Ron Paul. One was Pete Karpenko or "Captain Pete," as we used to call him.

Born in the Ukraine, Pete had fought in the czar's army against the Bolsheviks nearly a century ago. Pete did not fight for royalty or the aristocratic landowners. He did not fight to preserve the czar's hegemony over the Ukrainian people. He did not fight for capitalism. Pete fought simply because his family had worked hard, owned a few acres of land and they did not understand why the Bolsheviks wanted to take their land and give it to others—according to others' "need," not according to their work. Pete did not understand why if he and his family planted the land and reaped the harvest, why everyone else should share equally from the product.

Pete escaped to the United States once the Communists took over, and when I was a boy, he and I would play chess when he would come to visit my father. He played with the studiousness and thought process of an old warrior. I played like a kid fooling around with checkers, reckless and without forethought.

Over time, I've learned to think ahead about many things, not just chess. Socialism, by definition, is when the state takes control of major financial institutions and means of production.

With the federal government becoming involved in large parts of the private sector like banking and the auto industry in the last few years—all in the name of doing "good," of course—I began to worry. I worried about my kids. I worried about my hometown of Bowling Green and my home state of Kentucky. I worried about the direction of the entire country.

And I wasn't alone.

Who Is the Tea Party?

Tea Party supporters skew right politically; but demographically, they are generally representative of the public at large.
Gallup poll results, April 5, 2010

Critics and supporters alike often ask, "Who is the Tea Party?" Hundreds of thousands of folks across America have attended Tea Parties, separated by miles but united in their philosophy. Like Larry Hodge of Grayson County, who helped me get Sarah Palin's endorsement, and Dr. Lewis Hicks of Lexington, who helped me get Dr. James Dobson's endorsement, the Tea Partiers I met in Kentucky show the true face of this unprecedented and amazing grassroots movement.

Thomas and Rhonda Massie grew up in Lewis County. They excelled in school and eventually ended up at MIT. The Massies invented software involving virtual reality, which has been useful in robotic surgery, and formed a company that became a financial success. The Massies would eventually sell their company and move back to Kentucky. Thomas and Rhonda were big fans of Ron Paul and became early supporters of mine. It was a pleasure to meet them and I was humbled by their patriotism and concern for our future. Thomas was one of the many people who were motivated to run for office because of my father's presidential campaign. He ended up running for judge executive of Lewis County. He won.

Spencer and Kristen Bell are brother and sister. They were homeschooled. Spencer went to college at age twelve, and "took his time," graduating before he was eighteen. Both Spencer and Kristen were born into the liberty movement. Their dad, fresh out of college, traveled to Texas and volunteered for six months in my dad's first campaign in the 1970s. When I decided to run for Senate, Dale Bell ran into my father at a campaign event and said casually, "I've got two kids just out of college. Maybe they could come and help Rand?" And they did. Driving from Wyoming in January and staying until November, Spencer and Kristen Bell's help with my campaign was invaluable.

Early in the campaign, we received a call from Debbie Colburn, my seventeen-year-old son William's second-grade teacher. She wanted to let us know that her dad was a Republican and also a physician in Bell County, and she suggested that I call him. At the time I had never even been to Bell County. It is several hours from Bowling Green in the extreme southeast corner of Kentucky. Yet Dr. Meredith Evans became our county chairman and introduced me to most of the leaders of his community.

In northern Kentucky, our secret weapon was the Kunkel/ Bruggeman/Arlinghaus families or "clans." It has been said that 96 percent of Britain is related to Edward III. He had thirteen kids who lived to maturity and within a hundred years he had over four hundred descendants. The Kunkels/ Bruggemans/Arlinghauses had a few hundred relatives each. I joked that knowing a few good Catholic families in northern Kentucky gave me a lock on the election.

Big families aren't unusual in Kentucky. Senator Bunning's family alone has nine children and many grandchildren. One of the most heartwarming stories I heard during the campaign was Senator Bunning telling me that his wife's mother, who was over a hundred years old, had voted for me with an absentee ballot just days before her death. The Bunnings' support was unquestionably a big part of our victory.

In Harlan, Kentucky, I met the Rice family. Tim Rice owns a small welding business that does work in and for the coal industry. His father was a Barry Goldwater supporter. Tim told me he was a fan of Ayn Rand. He knew nearly everyone in and around Harlan and was related to most of the community. Tim had lost a brother in the coal mines but did not harbor bitterness, understanding the inherent dangers of mining. Tim still worked in the mines and understood how eastern Kentucky's past and future are intertwined with coal. Tim had learned of his brother's death when the owner of the mine came to their house with the sad news. Tim seemed to understand something I had tried to explain during the campaign: that we all want safety and we all want to avoid tragedy, but sometimes tragedies will inevitably occur. I tried to liken inherently hazardous occupations like mining to surgery where, sometimes, even if all precautions are taken, bad outcomes or even death occur. I tried to explain that sometimes tragedies are beyond our control. The media crucified me and tried to make me out to be some callous ideologue. The truth is that only someone who works in a dangerous occupation—mining, fire fighting, soldiering, police work—can fully grasp the serious decisions that are involved in such lines of work, each and every day.

Discussing serious issues in an adult and in-depth fashion

that ventured beyond sound bites was part of what characterized my campaign and was a primary reason so many concerned Kentuckians flocked to it. I'm amused when elitist critics try to paint the Tea Party as unintelligent given that it was my more mainstream opponents, in both the primary and general election, who chose to demagogue and talk down to voters with the same old bromides and clichés. In my experience, voters simply were not afraid to have serious conversations about entitlements, healthcare, education, over-regulation and, of course, spending and the debt.

As I work as a senator for Kentucky I carry with me many stories about the different Tea Party members I met, from all walks of life—young and old, black and white, business owners to coal miners—who inspired my campaign and delivered us victory. What I know and the country has seen is that the Tea Party represents our best chance in a long time of having intelligent discussions about the problems we face.

And I intend to continue those discussions in Congress.

Too Extreme?

Democratic attacks on Republicans and the Tea Party for being too extreme are failing to sway voters....
The Hill, October 19, 2010

No political party has a monopoly on hypocrisy; it seems to be a bipartisan trait. You see Republicans who wear their family values on their sleeves and run off with some intern or mistress. You see Democrats who preach about everyone paying their "fair share" of taxes, but once appointed to high office, we often learn that these politicians haven't been paying their *own* taxes.

Is it any wonder that Congress routinely gets an approval rating of 20 percent?

Is it any wonder that only 50 percent of eligible voters bother to register? And that only 50 percent of registered voters actually show up at the polls and vote? Add cynicism to hypocrisy and you capture the mind of many American voters. Why are voters cynical? Perhaps because Republicans have promised balanced budgets but instead doubled the size of the debt? Maybe because Democrats promised to help the working class but allowed fat cats on Wall Street to take home multimillion-dollar retention bonuses, for doing such a "great job." Now the Democrats are accelerating the debt at a faster rate than the Republicans—and faster than at any other time in our history.

Nobody trusts the government and America is broke, even as politicians behave otherwise.

Every time I think about our debt, I'm reminded of the famous newspaper letter response to a little girl who had asked if there was a Santa Claus. The paper responded that "Yes, Virginia there is a Santa Claus." I'm inclined to say, "No, Kentucky, or America, there is no Santa Claus," and it certainly isn't the federal government.

In Bowling Green, we received $1 million in federal stimulus. Local politicians, both Democrats and Republicans, jumped for joy, bragging about the many projects the stimulus dollars would buy. But no one asked the tough question: where did this money come from? Who will ultimately pay the bill? This year the federal deficit will be 13 percent of gross national product (GNP). Federal Spending will be 28 percent of GNP. We doubled our monetary base last year by increasing our money supply, at a rate greater than at any other time in modern history. This will cause inflation, as it always does, and when inflation is substantial it outpaces wages, hurting the working class and those on fixed incomes most—perhaps ironically, the demographics those most in favor of big government claim to be helping.

But to point out the obvious makes me or the Tea Party too "extreme," or so we are told. But what is extreme is a $2 trillion annual deficit. What is extreme is a budget that spends $383 billion on interest alone, more than we spend on all the roads in the United States.

Finally, is it extreme to balance our budget, live within our means and cut waste in government? Is it extreme to ask members of Congress to actually read their bills before voting? Politicians want to make me wait to buy a gun. Is it extreme for me to want to make them wait to pass a bill? Is it extreme to ask that we quit printing money out of thin air?

A New Politics

Though not the mainstream today, Rand Paul reflects a different age when professionals lent their expertise to government; when our officials were successful privately and applied their skills publicly as a civic virtue. Patrick Henry, Thomas Jefferson, John Adams, Benjamin Franklin, George Washington and many afterward have died, but left their example by which we should gauge our current and future officials. Rand Paul fits the mold.
Ryan Lees, Townhall.com

In the Senate, I will stand up and *force* a vote on having a balanced budget. Not some five-decade-long plan or promise to maybe, perhaps, possibly, consider doing this down the line, but a genuine balanced budget!

I will introduce a budget that balances in one year. If that fails, I will introduce one that balances in two years. If that fails, I will introduce a budget that will be balanced in three years—whatever it takes to get to a five-year balanced budget. And I will ask for a vote on each budget.

I will introduce a mandatory waiting period for every twenty pages in a bill, during which the Senate must wait one day in order to properly read and consider the proposal. Some say this might slow the rate of government growth or action. Exactly.

I will re-introduce the legislation that last year my father introduced in the House and Senators DeMint and Sanders introduced in the Senate to audit the Federal Reserve. Some say this might undermine the Fed's ability to print new money. Exactly.

Whether or not I will vote to raise the debt ceiling is already being bandied about. When Newt Gingrich and congressional Republicans shut down the government in 1994 it was a loss, public-relations-wise, so I will propose another alternative. If the Democrats want to make it a choice between either raising the debt ceiling or shutting down government, how about we don't raise the debt ceiling and fund government based on receivables? We bring in over $2 trillion per year, about $200 billion a month or nearly $7 billion dollars in revenue a day. Can't we simply have an austerity plan that funds government on what the government collects until the recession ends?

I will introduce a $500 billion spending cut bill, much of

it based on *Heritage Foundation* analyst Brian Riedl's plan to cut $343 billion from our federal budget, examined in the previous chapter.

We must begin to sunset government regulations. Let them expire unless Congress reapproves them. Burdensome and often unnecessary regulations drain the economy to the tune of approximately $1 trillion per year, and most are written or devised by unelected bureaucrats. Sen. Lisa Murkowski recently introduced legislation that might limit the Environmental Protection Agency's authority to impose such regulations. Murkowski's bill failed, but she made the point that: "It should be up to us to set the policy of this country, not unelected bureaucrats within an agency." I agree and will work with her and other senators toward rectifying this wrong. Glenn Beck has noted that you can't be for job creation and against job creators, and neither American businesspeople nor taxpayers deserve many of these intrusive and costly regulations.

The president's debt commission has mentioned entitlement reform. This is something I talked about throughout my campaign and the Tea Party now drives the debate over entitlement reform, showing that the public is ready for honest solutions. It also shows that the typical "Mediscare" ads are no longer working. The time is ripe to finally address this pressing issue and I look forward to working with anyone from either side of the aisle serious about doing so.

I believe big money in politics has been, and is, part of the reason our deficit is out of control. Previous attempts at campaign finance reform have failed because they did not understand that political speech is nevertheless speech. I agreed with Senator McConnell and the Supreme Court that McCain–Feingold was unconstitutional. I do, however, believe that we can place contractual, voluntarily accepted limits on any corporation or entity that signs a federal contract. I will propose that any federal contracts over a million dollars include a clause that precludes that entity from PAC contributions and lobbying.

I will vote to institute term limits.

I will not vote for a tax increase.

I will not vote for earmarks.

I will not vote for an unbalanced budget.

I will not vote to go to war without a formal declaration of war, as our soldiers deserve and the Constitution demands.

My legislative proposals and suggestions outlined here are just the beginning of an always evolving and ongoing plan to bring real reform to Washington, DC. It was the Tea Party that got me to Capitol Hill and it will be the movement and its spirit that will drive and inspire me in the ongoing battle to take our government back.

I Have a Message

Eternal vigilance is the price of liberty.
Thomas Jefferson

As candidate, nominee, and now Senator, I have always had a message. It is a message from the Tea Party, and a message that is loud and clear and does not mince words.

We've come to take our government back!

Career politicians of all stripes and persuasions have sold us down the river with false promises, with the illusion that real wealth can come to a country that chronically spends more than it takes in, borrows, and prints money to pay the difference.

We must now take our government back—back from the special interests, the lobbyists, and the pork barrel spendthrifts who are bankrupting this great nation. No more deficits. No more bailouts. Our government has taxed us beyond belief, and with its profligate ways has borrowed and borrowed to a degree that now burdens future generations.

We've had enough. Our system of government is broken. Where once we had a government restrained by the Constitution, we now have politicians who see their power as unlimited, with massive spending occurring no matter which party is in power.

I am galled by the politicians who prance around with oversized checks, often emblazoned with their signatures, as if they expect us to believe that in bringing home the pork the money came from them personally. I promised at every stop in every city not to bring home the bacon. I told the voters of Kentucky that the pig was picked clean, that I would not borrow money from China or clamor to bring more dollars borrowed from overseas home to my state.

But I will fight to make sure taxpayers keep more of their own money. I will never forget that it is your labor, your sweat and your tears that earned you *your* money. Politicians should not forever be sticking their hands in citizens' wallets, insisting that it's good for us—when too often the only person it's truly good for is the politician.

The Tea Party movement arose in response to our impending debt and has created an environment in which everything under the sun—taxes, spending, entitlements, healthcare, foreign policy, domestic policy—can now be re-examined, reconsidered or perhaps even rejected, in the name of returning to limited, constitutional government. Republicans and Democrats alike now know that if they attempt to play the same old politics, the Tea Party possesses the influence and power to make life tough for politicians who insist on business-as-usual.

And this is only the beginning. Critics have been predicting the Tea Party's demise since its inception, and yet after two or three years, two or three elections, as the movement continues to make waves and continues to turn the tide, we've proven we're here to stay. Believe me, the establishment is definitely getting the Tea Party's message—whether it likes it or not.

It is the Tea Party that now shapes our politics. When the president and the Democrats see the need to appoint a debt commission, it is the Tea Party that is setting the agenda. When Republicans begin talking more than they once did about cutting spending and earmarks, it is the Tea Party that now has their ear.

We must make sure that Washington keeps listening. The worst thing that could possibly happen is for the Tea Party to build a movement powerful enough to influence politics and win elections and then rest on its laurels after only a few wins. Elections are just the beginning, and we must hold politicians' feet to the fire, demanding that they do what we sent them to Washington to do. We need more citizen-statesmen, as the Founders intended, and fewer career politicians. There are plenty of politicians who would simply love to go back to business as usual without any pesky Tea Partiers messing up their status quo agenda. We can't let that happen.

Politicians inside the Beltway have said they will co-opt the Tea Party, and that the movement will wilt and wither under their tutelage. On national television I responded, "We're loud, we're proud and we will co-opt them!" The Tea Party won its first battle over earmarks even before the new Congress was sworn in. Since many of the new Tea Party Senators are first-time office holders, we are not yet beaten down by the system. We believe we can change the world.

My father has always said that we wouldn't have all these problems if our leaders would simply do what they swore to do, and just follow the Constitution. He's right. The answer to so many of today's problems lies in no longer debating what politicians should do—but insisting on what they must do.

The Constitution is very clear about it. The Tea Party's job is to keep making things clearer, and this is only the beginning. It is not a job that will be finished overnight or even in an election cycle.

Thomas Jefferson believed that the price of liberty was eternal vigilance—and now the Tea Party must prove it.

Suggestions for Further Reading

Must-read classics in the cause of liberty:

- *The Road to Serfdom*, Friedrich A. Hayek
- *The Conscience of a Conservative*, Barry Goldwater
- *Human Action*, Ludwig von Mises
- *Conceived in Liberty*, Murray N. Rothbard
- *Atlas Shrugged*, Ayn Rand

Drawn from his lifelong fight for limited government, my father's books remain indispensable for conservatives:

- *The Revolution: A Manifesto*, Ron Paul
- *End the Fed*, Ron Paul
- *A Foreign Policy of Freedom*, Ron Paul

Valuable books offering a better understanding of our economic instability:

- *Meltdown: A Free-Market Look at Why the Stock Market Collapsed, the Economy Tanked, and Government Bailouts Will Make Things Worse*, Thomas E. Woods Jr.

- *The Politically Incorrect Guide to the Great Depression and the New Deal*, Robert P. Murphy
- *Broke: The Plan to Restore Our Trust, Truth and Treasure*, Glenn Beck
- *Economics in One Lesson*, Henry Hazlitt

Great guides toward returning to the Constitution and how the Tea Party now leads this fight:

- *Who Killed the Constitution?: The Fate of American Liberty from World War I to George W. Bush*, Thomas E. Woods Jr. and Kevin R. C. Gutzman
- *The Constitution in Exile: How the Federal Government Has Seized Power by Rewriting the Supreme Law of the Land*, Andrew P. Napolitano
- *Red State Uprising: How to Take America Back*, Erick Erickson and Lewis K. Uhler
- *The Last Best Hope: Restoring Conservatism and America's Promise*, Joe Scarborough

Recommended reading for a more rational, affordable, and traditionally conservative foreign policy based on real defense and genuine national interests:

- *The New American Militarism: How Americans Are Seduced by War*, Andrew J. Bacevich
- *Blowback: The Costs and Consequences of American Empire*, Chalmers Johnson
- *Imperial Hubris: Why the West Is Losing the War on Terror*, Michael Scheuer

- *Where the Right Went Wrong: How Neoconservatives Subverted the Reagan Revolution and Hijacked the Bush Presidency*, Patrick J. Buchanan
- *Silent Night: The Remarkable Christmas Truce of 1914*, Stanley Weintraub

Classic novels:

- *The Brothers Karamazov* and *Crime and Punishment*, Fyodor Dostoyevsky
- *All Quiet on the Western Front*, Erich Maria Remarque

Suggested Websites and Organizations:

- **The Cato Institute:** The leading libertarian think tank in Washington, DC, and a great source for liberty-oriented information and thought: www.cato.org
- **The Heritage Foundation:** The leading conservative think tank in Washington, DC, and a great source for conservative information and thought: www.heritage.org
- **Campaign for Liberty:** Founded by Ron Paul and one of the fastest-growing organizations promoting political and economic liberty through education and activism: www.campaignforliberty.com
- **Young Americans for Liberty:** America's fastest-growing and most effective liberty-minded youth/student organization, with over 500 chapters in colleges and high schools: www.yaliberty.org
- **The Ludwig von Mises Institute:** Home of the world's best free market economists of the Austrian school. An

indispensable aid in promoting capitalism and rejecting socialism: www.mises.org

- **The American Conservative:** Founded by Pat Buchanan, this magazine for "thinking conservatives" regularly challenges not only the Left but the neoconservatives and big government Republicans: www.amconmag.com
- **Red State:** The leading conservative news blog for right-of-center online activists: www.redstate.com
- **The 9-12 Project:** Inspired by Glenn Beck, this group continues to organize at the grass-roots level to ensure that American liberty and freedom may endure: www.the912project.com
- **Northern Kentucky Tea Party:** One of Kentucky's many growing and influential Tea Parties that helped deliver my victory: www.nkyteaparty.org
- **Tea Party Express:** An ongoing Tea Party bus tour taking the message of fiscal sanity nationwide, one city at a time: www.teapartyexpress.org
- **Freedom Works:** Dick Armey's Freedom Works fights for lower taxes, less government, and more economic freedom for all Americans: www.freedomworks.org
- **Tea Party Patriots:** Fighting for fiscal responsibility, limited government, and free markets: www.teapartypatriots.org

I have graciously received permission from the following authors to quote their original material in the book: James Antle, Doug Bandow, Fred Barnes, Bruce Bartlett, Pat Buchanan, Michael Burry, Conn Carroll, Neil Cavuto, Patrick Chisolm, Senator Tom Coburn, Andrew Coulson, Janice Shaw Crouse, Senator Jim DeMint, E. J. Dionne, Thomas Donnelly, Daniel Drezner, Peter Ferrara, Phillip Giraldi, Ryan Lees, Robert Pape, Danielle Pletka, Scott Rasmussen, Brian Riedl, Michael Rozeff, Peter Schiff, Douglas Schoen, Michael Tanner, Stephen Walt, and Matt Welch

And the following publications have granted permission: Americans for Tax Reform, *The Enquirer*

The copyrighted photos in the book are used with permission from the following: Cody Duty (page x); Michael Nystrom, revolutionaryposters.com (page 2); The Paul Family Collection (page 24); Walter Gilbert, polipix.posterous.com (page 46); AP Photo/Ed Reinke (pages 66, 106): Joe Imel/ Daily News (pages 90, 170): The Strategy Group for Media (pages 130, 194); Gage Skidmore (page 216); Getty Images/ Chip Somodevilla (page 236)